Mathematics
Olympiad

Class 06

Mathematics Olympiad

Class 06

A must have book for all
Olympiads & Talent Search Exams...

by
Akash Deep

BLOOM CAP
Bloom Cap Edu Ventures Pvt. Ltd.

Bloom Cap Edu Ventures Pvt. Ltd.

卐 **Administrative & Production Office**

'Ramchhaya' 4577/15, Agarwal Road, Darya Ganj, New Delhi -110002
Tele: 011- 47630600, 43518550

卐 **ISBN :** 978-93-25519-15-2

卐 **PRICE :** ₹100.00

卐 **PO No :** TXT-XX-XXXXXXX-X-XX

For further information about the books log on to
www.bloomcap.org

Follow us on   

Preface

"Future belongs to those Who prepares for it today"

School Olympiads are National & International level competitions conducted by different Government, Non-Government & Educational Organisations with the purpose of making the children ready to face competitive exams. The challenging Questions asked in Olympiads motivate them to learn more & more and bring out the best result with improved academic performance. The Awards & Scholarship offered in Olympiads motivate children to aspire & strive for doing better and emerge out to be the best.

Maths Olympiads

Mathematics is an integral part of all competitive exams be it Aptitude or Commerce or Science. Maths Olympiads are meant to develop Mathematical aptitude in school students. They provide students with an opportunity to master their concepts and comprehend tricky questions effortlessly. Challenging Questions of Maths Olympiads encourage students to develop a logical approach to solve Mathematical Problems.

'Bloom Mathematics Olympiad Study Book Class 6' is a perfect resource to Study & Practice for Olympiad Exams and other National & State Level Talent Search Exams & Other Competitions.

Some Special Features of Bloom Maths Olympiad Study Books are;

- Chapterwise Exercises having different types of Objective Questions at par with the Olympiad Level.
- Detailed Explanation for each question.
- Olympiad Pattern Practice Sets at the end.

This book is prepared by Expert Panel with the utmost care, still if you have any suggestions regarding its improvement, then feel free to contact us at olympiads@bloomcap.org. We will try to inculcate your suggestions in the further editions.

Contents

01.	Numbers	1-4
02.	Whole Numbers	5-7
03.	Integers	8-10
04.	Fractions	11-14
05.	Decimals	15-17
06.	Ratio and Proportion	18-19
07.	Algebra	20-22
08.	Elementary Shapes	23-26
09.	Geometry	27-30
10.	Symmetry	31-34
11.	Mensuration	35-38
12.	Data Handling	39-43
•	**Practice Set 1**	**44-48**
•	**Practice Set 2**	**49-53**
•	**Hints & Solutions**	**54-90**

Numbers

1 Mark Questions

1. Which of the following number is written according to the international system of numeration?
   (a) 18,32,480
   (b) 1,832,480
   (c) 1,83,24,80
   (d) None of these

2. Which of the following is the greatest number with 7 at the hundreds place?
   (a) 1798   (b) 9817   (c) 9781   (d) 7981

3. What is the difference between the place value and face value of 5 in 79502?
   (a) 500
   (b) 95
   (c) 495
   (d) 0

4. The greatest and smallest 4-digit numbers formed by using the digits 5, 0, 2 and 6 are
   (a) 5260, 5206
   (b) 2560, 2650
   (c) 6520, 2056
   (d) 6502, 2506

5. What is the greatest 5-digit number formed by the digits 2, 7, 8, 9 and 0 without repetition of digits?
   (a) 27890
   (b) 09782
   (c) 98720
   (d) 89720

6. Choose the correct expanded form of 69046.
   (a) $60000 + 9000 + 400 + 60$
   (b) $60000 + 900 + 40 + 6$
   (c) $60000 + 9000 + 40 + 6$
   (d) $60000 + 900 + 400 + 60$

7. How many millions are there in 85423610?
   (a) 8
   (b) 85
   (c) 80000000
   (d) 85000000

8. Follow the pattern given below and select the missing number.
     I. 26741, 21748, 27814, 24178 = 21748
    II. 47238, 42738, 42387, 43782 = 42387
   III. 92173, 92731, 97321, 91732 = 91732
   Then, 89426, 82946, 82469, 86429 = ?
   (a) 89426   (b) 82946   (c) 82469   (d) 86429

9. Fill in the blanks with the help of options, given below :
     (i) C   (ii) Face   (iii) 10
    (iv) 100   (v) Width   (vi) Period
   (vii) 1000   (viii) Place   (ix) I
     I. Commas are inserted in a number after each _____.
    II. The first basic roman numeral is _____.
   III. _____ value of a number is the number itself.
   IV. 1000 = _____ hundred.
    V. 1 lakh = _____ thousand.
   Codes
         I   II   III   IV   V
   (a) (v)   (i)   (viii)   (iv)   (iii)
   (b) (vi)   (ix)   (ii)   (iii)   (iv)
   (c) (vi)   (i)   (ii)   (iv)   (iii)
   (d) (v)   (ix)   (ii)   (iii)   (iv)

10. Estimating the difference of $11793 - 9372$ by rounding off each number to nearest hundreds, we get

(a) 2400   (b) 2500
(c) 2421   (d) 2521

11. Estimating the product of 3239×38 by rounding off each number to nearest tens, we get

(a) 123080   (b) 123082
(c) 129622   (d) 129600

12. Choose the incorrect match.

	Column A	Column B
I.	72946 rounded off to nearest thousand is	73000
II.	46230 rounded off to nearest thousand is	46000
III.	58996 rounded off to nearest thousand is	58000
IV.	62341 rounded off to nearest thousand is	62000

Codes

(a) I   (b) II
(c) III   (d) IV

13. The imports of the country in the year 2014 are estimated as 746493 units whereas exports are estimated as 634629 units. Find the difference in exports and imports by rounding off import and export to nearest thousands.

(a) 111864   (b) 112000
(c) 111000   (d) 110000

14. Difference of 600 and 200 is :

(a) CCCC   (b) CD
(c) DM   (d) D

15. The difference between the smallest 3-digit and greatest 2-digit numbers in roman can be written as

(a) I   (b) XX
(c) XC   (d) C

16. Meenakshi's date of joining her job is 29th December. Express the date in Roman numerals.

(a) XXIX   (b) XIX
(c) XIXX   (d) IXXX

17. Find the correct descending order of XIX, XCIX, LXXV.

(a) XIX, LXXV, XCIX   (b) XCIX, LXXV, XIX
(c) LXXV, XCIX, XIX   (d) XCIX, XIX, LXXV

18. 55 m 20 cm of cloth is being used to make 15 shirts. The length of cloth used to make one such shirt is

(a) 3 m 20 cm   (b) 400 cm
(c) 3 m 68 cm   (d) 488 cm

19. An abundant number is less than the sum of its factors (other than itself). Which is the least abundant number?

(a) 8   (b) 12
(c) 15   (d) 18

20. Which number is a factor of 20 but not a multiple of 2?

(a) 12   (b) 5
(c) 4   (d) 10

21. The number of multiples of both 3 and 5 in the first 100 natural numbers is

(a) 9   (b) 10
(c) 6   (d) 7

22. If a is the factor of b and c is the multiple of b, then which of the following is true?

(a) a divides c (b) c divides b
(c) $a \times b = c$ (d) $b \div a = c$

23. The sum of two prime numbers is 39. What is the product of these numbers?

(a) 15   (b) 72
(c) 74   (d) 63

24. The composite number with exactly 4 factors is

(a) 16   (b) 14
(c) 18   (d) None of these

25. The greatest number which can divide 33, 63 and 75 leaving the same remainder 3 in each cases, is

(a) 6   (b) 12   (c) 15   (d) 26

26. Micheal and Martin collect hockey cards. Micheal has 45 cards in his collection and Martin has 30 cards in his collection. If the cards in collection of both boys come in packages of the same number of cards, then how many cards of each of them can be packed of equal numbers?

(a) 15

(b) 30

(c) 45

(d) Can't be determined

27. **Assertion** (A) LCM of 23 and 29 is 1.

Reason (R) LCM of two coprime numbers is their product.

(a) (A) is true and (R) is the correct explanation of (A).

(b) (A) is false and (R) is the correct explanation of (A).

(c) (A) is true and (R) is false.

(d) Both (A) and (R) are false.

28. Fill in the blanks with the help of options given below:

(i) 1

(ii) Number itself

(iii) Composite numbers

(iv) Prime numbers

(v) xy

(vi) $x + y$

(vii) Factors

(viii) Multiples

    I. The numbers which have more than two factors are called __________.

   II. HCF of two coprime numbers is __________.

  III. The numbers which have only two factors (1 and itself) are called __________.

  IV. The LCM of a number is x and HCF is y, then product of numbers is __________.

Codes

	I	II	III	IV
(a)	(vii)	(i)	(iv)	(v)
(b)	(iv)	(ii)	(iii)	(vi)
(c)	(iii)	(i)	(iv)	(v)
(d)	(viii)	(ii)	(iii)	(vi)

29. Match the following.

Column A		Column B
I. Smallest prime number is	(i)	odd
II. Number whose general form is $2n+1$, is	(ii)	one
III. HCF of two or more prime numbers is	(iii)	even
IV. A number which has no multiples, is	(iv)	zero

Codes

	I	II	III	IV
(a)	(i)	(ii)	(iii)	(iv)
(b)	(ii)	(iii)	(iv)	(i)
(c)	(iii)	(i)	(ii)	(iv)
(d)	(iv)	(iii)	(ii)	(i)

30. In the sports day programme, the number of participants in football, basketball and running are 60, 84 and 108 respectively. The minimum number of rest rooms required, where in each room the same number of participants are to be seated and all of them being in the same sport are

(a) 20   (b) 22   (c) 25   (d) 21

2 Marks Questions

31. The HCF and LCM of two numbers are 46 and 368 respectively. If the first number when divided by 2 gives 46 as quotient and 0 as remainder, then the other number is

(a) 146   (b) 184
(c) 192   (d) 204

32. Place value of 5 in a 5-digit number is 5000 and place value of 3 in that number is 6 times of the place value of 5. Find the number.

(a) 53000   (b) 50030
(c) 35000   (d) 30050

33. The difference between the place values of digit 6 in the greatest and the smallest 5-digit number formed by using the digits 3, 1, 2, 8 and 6 (each digit should be used only once) is ....

(a) 760842
(b) 59940
(c) 999
(d) 5940

34. Moni needs to pack pencil boxes in a wooden box to carry to his school. If 50 of such pencil boxes weight 1 kg 250 gm, then how many such pencil boxes can come in a wooden box which has the capacity of 800 gm ?

(a) 40   (b) 38
(c) 34   (d) 32

35. Read the following statements carefully and select the correct option.

Statement I If a number is divisible by another number, then it is divisible by each of the factors of that number.

Statement II The least number which when divided by 12, 15, 20 and 27 leaves remainder 8, 11, 16 and 23 respectively is 536.

(a) Statement I is true but Statement II is false.
(b) Statement I is false but Statement II is true.
(c) Both Statement I and Statement II are true.
(d) Both Statement I and Statement II are false.

36. A number is completely divisible by 7 but when it is divided by 2, 3, 4, 5 and 6 respectively, it leaves a remainder of 1. The smallest such possible number is ....

(a) 301   (b) 302   (c) 308   (d) 315

37. There are 35 flats in Building A and 55 flats in Building B. If the cost of each flat in Building A and Building B is ₹ 25680 and ₹ 302800 respectively, then what is the difference between the cost of all the flats in Building A and Building B?

(a) ₹ 1375000   (b) ₹ 157550000
(c) ₹ 166540000   (d) ₹ 15755200

Chapter 02

Whole Numbers

1 Mark Questions

1. Consider the following statements.
   I. All whole numbers are natural numbers.
   II. Zero is the smallest whole number.
   III. 0 is not a natural number.
   Which of the statements are true?
   (a) I and II
   (b) I and III
   (c) II and III
   (d) All of these

2. The following figure represents the whole numbers. The point B represents which whole number?

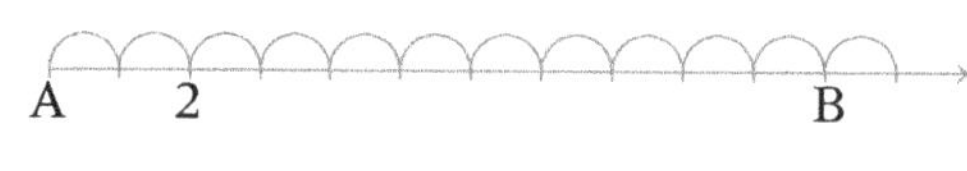

   (a) 7   (b) 13
   (c) 9   (d) 11

3. What does the following number line represents?

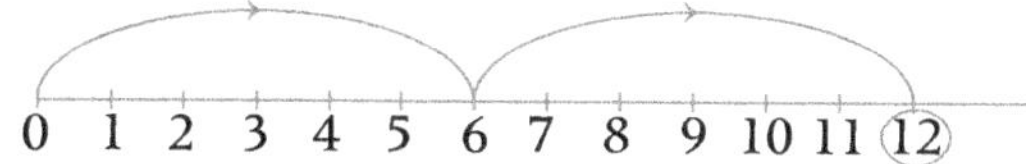

   (a) Addition of 0 and 12.
   (b) Subtraction of 0 and 12.
   (c) Multiplication of 6 and 2.
   (d) Multiplication of 6 and 6.

4. If $\dfrac{a}{b} = 0$, then which of the following is true?
   (a) $a = 0$
   (b) $b = 0$
   (c) Either $a = 0$ or $b = 0$
   (d) Neither $a = 0$ nor $b = 0$

5. The predecessor of 1 million will be equal to
   (a) 1000001   (b) 999999
   (c) 9999990   (d) 100001

6. The three consecutive whole numbers that come just before 7510001 are
   (a) 7510098, 7510099, 7510100
   (b) 7510008, 7510999, 7511000
   (c) 7509998, 7509999, 7510000
   (d) 7519998, 7519999, 7510000

7. The product of successor and predecessor of 199 is
   (a) 36900   (b) 39600
   (c) 3990   (d) 39900

8. What is the successor of predecessor of 1 lakh?
   (a) 99999   (b) 100001
   (c) 100000   (d) 99998

9. Which of the following properties is not satisfied by whole numbers under multiplication?
   (a) Closure property
   (b) Commutative property
   (c) Associative property
   (d) All of the above

10. If p and q are two whole numbers, then the commutative property is applicable to subtraction if and only if
    (a) $p = q$ (b) $p > q$ (c) $p < q$ (d) $p \neq q$

11. Which of the option is an example of commutative property?
    (a) $30 \times 1 = 30$
    (b) $4 \times (2 + 3) = 4 \times 2 + 4 \times 3$
    (c) $14 + 16 = 16 + 14$
    (d) $12 + 0 = 12$

12. $72(7 + 3) = 72 \times 7 + 72 \times 3$ is an example of which of the following property?
    (a) Closure   (b) Associative
    (c) Commutative   (d) Distributive

13. Write the product in form of distributive property.
    $$129 \times 30 + 129 \times 10$$
    (a) $129(30 + 10)$ (b) 139×30
    (c) 40×129 (d) $(120 + 10) \times 30$

14. Match the following columns.

Column A	Column B
I. 5 + 6 is a whole number	(i) Additive identity
II. $12 \times (15 \times 9)$ $= (12 \times 15) \times 9$	(ii) Associative property
III. $14 \times (20 - 1)$ $= 14 \times 20 - 14 \times 1$	(iii) Commutative property
IV. $14 \times 16 = 16 \times 14$	(iv) Closed under addition property
V. 1 is called the	(v) Distributive property
VI. 0 is called the	(iv) Multiplicative identity

Codes

    I II III IV V VI
(a) (i) (ii) (iii) (iv) (v) (vi)
(b) (ii) (i) (iii) (iv) (v) (vi)
(c) (iv) (ii) (v) (iii) (vi) (i)
(d) (iii) (iv) (ii) (v) (i) (vi)

15. Madonna has a picture that she wants to frame. The cost is ₹ 17 plus an amount that depends on the length of framing needed. The man in the shop says it will cost ₹ 17, plus ₹ 5 on each per cm. If the length of frame is 15 cm, then which expression expresses the cost of frame?
    (a) $17 + (5 \times 15)$
    (b) $17 \times 5 + 15$
    (c) $(17 + 5) \times 15$
    (d) $17 + 5 + 15$

16. A shopkeeper sold 40 milk packets on Monday. The next day, he sold 60 milk packets. If the cost of one packet of milk is ₹ 25, then which of the following will be the correct expression?
    (a) $25 \times (40 + 60)$
    (b) $25 + (40 \times 60)$
    (c) $25 + 60 + 40$
    (d) None of these

17. If $5476a$ is divisible by 3, then what can be the value of a?
    (a) 1   (b) 2   (c) 3   (d) 6

18. Consider the following statements and choose the correct option(s) for them.
    I. A number divisible by 3 is also divisible by 9.
    II. A number divisible by 3 and by 9, if the sum of all its digits can be divided by 3 and by 9, respectively.

Codes
    (a) I is true.
    (b) II is true.
    (c) Both I and II are true.
    (d) Neither I nor II is true.

19. What least value should be given to *, so that the number 234 * 65 is divisible by 11?
(a) 5
(b) 7
(c) 11
(d) None of the above

20. Find the number of dots in pattern 50?

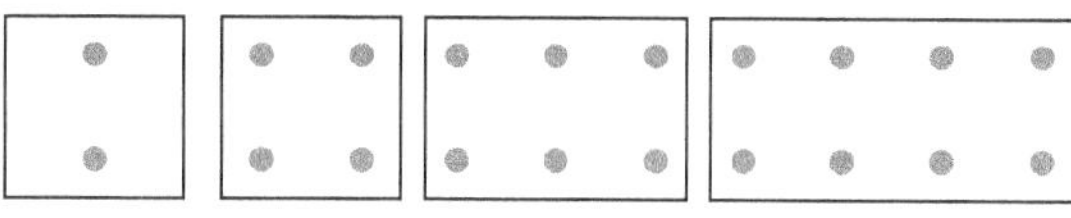

(a) 50
(b) 100
(c) 200
(d) 25

2 Marks Questions

21. Which of the following statements are not correct?
 I. Whole numbers are closed under multiplication.
 II. Whole numbers are closed under subtraction.
 III. The commutative property is true under addition for whole numbers.
 IV. The commutative property is true under division for whole numbers.

Codes
(a) I and II
(b) II and III
(c) I and III
(d) II and IV

22. Ritika makes 18 gift packs containing chocolates for Diwali. She puts 12 vanilla chocolates, 14 milk chocolates and 8 nut chocolates in each pack. With the help of which property, can you calculate the total number of chocolates in 18 packs?
(a) Commutative property
(b) Associative property
(c) Distributive property
(d) None of the above

23. A 6-digit number begins with the digit 8. The number is divisible by 9. All the digits of the number are different. What is the smallest possible value of this number?
(a) 810234
(b) 801234
(c) 812340
(d) None of the above

24. If a 4-digit number A is divisible by 3, then which of the following is correct?
(a) Reverse of the number is also divisible by 3.
(b) Reverse of the number is not divisible by 3.
(c) Interchanging the number of odd and even places still make the number divisible by 3.
(d) None of the above

25. A is the smallest three digit number which leaves a remainder 2 when divided by 17. B is the smallest three digit number which leaves remainder 7 when divided by 12. Then $A + B$ is
(a) 312
(b) 219
(c) 205
(d) 207

Integers

1 Mark Questions

1. Ajay went to Leh and recorded the temperature as $-3°C$. What is the equivalent way of saying it?
   (a) 3°C below 0°C
   (b) 3°C above 0°C
   (c) 3°C above 100°C
   (d) 3°C below 100°C

2. Choose the correct option on the basis of below number line.

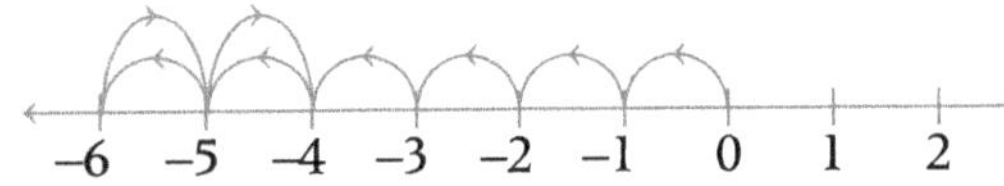

   (a) $0 + 6 + 4$
   (b) $0 - 6 + 4$
   (c) $0 + 6 - 2$
   (d) $0 - 6 + 2$

3. 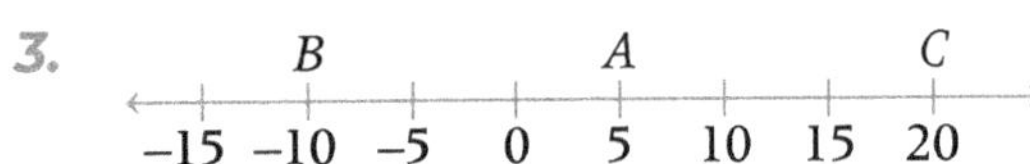

   The above diagram shows a number line. The value of $A - (B) + C$ is equal to
   (a) -15 (b) 35 (c) 20 (d) -10

4. Which of the following represents a negative integer?
   (a) A bird is flying at a height of 40 m above the ground.
   (b) Northern pine snakes hibernate at depth between 20 and 42 inches.
   (c) A deposit of ₹ 4000 in the bank.
   (d) Ashish travelled 10 km towards East to reach his destination.

5. Choose the correct statement.
   (a) If the dividend and divisor have unlike sign, then the quotient will be negative.
   (b) If the two factors of a number are of like sign, then their product is positive.
   (c) If the addends are of same sign, then the sign of their sum is the same as the sign of the addends.
   (d) All of the above

6. Which expression has closest value to 0?
   (a) $26 - 24$
   (b) $24 - (-29)$
   (c) $-30 + 31$
   (d) $-2 - 6$

7. Sum of two integers is -35. If one of them is 15, then other one is
   (a) $+20$ (b) -20
   (c) -50 (d) $+50$

8. Choose the correct statement when a negative integer a is subtracted from another negative integer b such that $a > b$, then the sign of the result is
   (a) always negative
   (b) always positive
   (c) never negative
   (d) Can't be determined

9. Siddharth and Roop visited two places A and B respectively in Jammu and recorded the minimum temperatures at a particular day as $-5°C$ at A and $-2°C$ at B. Which of the following statements is true?
   (a) A is cooler than B.
   (b) B is cooler than A.
   (c) There is a difference of $7°C$ in the temperature.
   (d) None of the above

10. Ammonium nitrate is a chemical used to lower the temperature of water. The temperature of solution A changes from $10°C$ to $-16°C$ when 1 part of ammonium nitrate and 1 part of water are added. What is the change in temperature occurred?
    (a) Fall by $4°C$
    (b) Fall by $26°C$
    (c) Fall by $6°C$
    (d) Fall by $-20\ °C$

11. Find the sum of largest 5-digit even positive integer and the largest 5-digit odd negative integer.
    (a) 89997
    (b) 89999
    (c) 80009
    (d) 10009

12. An architectural drawing of a building of an office shows elevation of the basement floor to be -14 ft. The elevation of the roof is 23 ft. What is the total distance from the roof to the basement floor?
    (a) 7 ft　　　　　　(b) 12 ft
    (c) 28 ft　　　　　(d) 37 ft

13. Langkawi cable care upon reaching the middle station reaches a height of 650 m above sea level although the top station is at an altitude of 708 m from the sea level. How can we represent the above heights respectively?
    (a) -650 m and -708 m
    (b) -650 m and 708 m
    (c) 650 m and -700 m
    (d) 650 m and 708 m

14. In 2010, Ganesh fund lost ₹ 9000. In 2011, it lost another ₹ 10000 and in 2012, it lost ₹ 17000. In 2013, it gained ₹ 16000 and in 2014, it gained ₹ 12000. How much does he have at the end?
    (a) Loss of ₹ 2000　　(b) Gain of ₹ 5000
    (c) Loss of ₹ 8000　　(d) Gain of ₹ 10000

15. Simplify and choose the correct option.
    $2 - [\{1 + (4 - 7) - 8\} - 9]$
    (a) 20　　(b) -19　　(c) -23　　(d) 21

2 Marks Questions

16. State 'T' for true and 'F' for false.

    I. -7 is on the right side of -4 on the number line.

    II. The additive inverse of a negative integer is positive.

    III. The integer 5 is located to the right of -4.

    IV. A loss of ₹ 400 is denoted by ₹(-400).

Codes

	I	II	III	IV
(a)	F	T	T	T
(b)	T	T	T	T
(c)	F	F	F	T
(d)	T	F	F	T

17. Fill in the blanks with the help of options given in the box.

(i) Seven	(ii) Negative
(iii) Six	(iv) -31
(v) Positive	(vi) $=$
(vii) $<$	(viii) Zero
(ix) -30	(x) $\dfrac{1}{0}$

    I. _______ integers are there between -8 and -1.

    II. Every integer less than zero is _______.

    III. The successor of predecessor of -30 is _______.

    IV. $|(-11) + (-15)|$ _______ $(11) + (15)$

    V. The additive inverse of zero is _______.

Codes

	I	II	III	IV	V
(a)	(i)	(v)	(iv)	(vii)	(viii)
(b)	(iii)	(v)	(ix)	(vii)	(x)
(c)	(i)	(ii)	(iv)	(vi)	(x)
(d)	(iii)	(ii)	(ix)	(vi)	(viii)

Directions (Q. Nos. 18-20) The following table lists the daily fluctuations of the Dow Jones Industrial Average under US stock market.

September 22	-107
September 23	-117
September 24	155
September 25	-265
September 26	168
September 29	-42
September 30	-29
October 1	-238
October 2	-3
October 3 (12 : 45 pm EST)	200
Average	132

18. What is lowest point to which it falled in the given 10 days?

    (a) -238 (b) -3

    (c) 200   (d) -265

19. What is the increase/decrease of points on comparing the days September 25 and October 1?

    (a) Increase of 27 points

    (b) Decrease of 27 points

    (c) Increase of 30 points

    (d) Decrease of 30 points

20. What is the difference between the highest and lowest points achieved in these given days?

    (a) 65   (b) -65

    (c) -465 (d) 465

Fractions

1 Mark Questions

1. 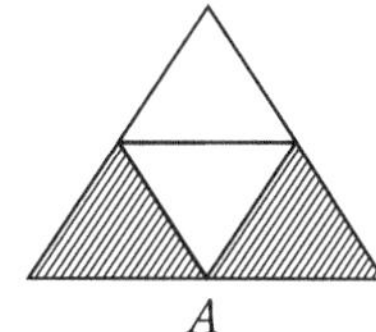 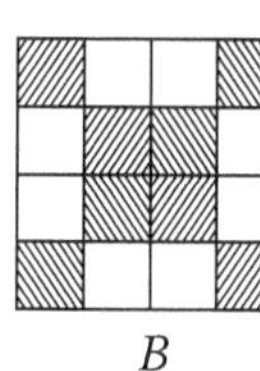

A

B

From the above figures, we can say that A and B represent

(a) Equivalent fraction

(b) Improper fraction

(c) Like fraction

(d) None of the above

2. Find the missing number. $3\dfrac{4}{7} = \dfrac{\square}{14}$

(a) 21 (b) 25

(c) 30 (d) 50

3. Four friends shared 5 pancakes. How much did each one get?

(a) $\dfrac{4}{5}$ (b) $\dfrac{1}{5}$ (c) $\dfrac{5}{4}$ (d) $\dfrac{1}{4}$

4. State 'T' for true and 'F' for false.

I. A number representing a whole part is called a fraction.

II. $13\dfrac{5}{18}$ is a proper fraction.

III. An improper fraction can be converted into a mixed fraction.

IV. Fractions having same numerator are called like fractions.

Codes

	I	II	III	IV
(a)	F	F	T	F
(b)	T	T	F	F
(c)	F	F	T	T
(d)	F	T	F	T

5. What fraction will come in place of * ?

$$\dfrac{1}{8},\ \dfrac{2}{27},\ \dfrac{3}{64},\ \dfrac{4}{125},\ *,\ \dfrac{6}{343}$$

(a) $\dfrac{5}{250}$ (b) $\dfrac{5}{216}$

(c) $\dfrac{5}{313}$ (d) $\dfrac{4}{261}$

6. Which of the following fractions is not equivalent to $\dfrac{1}{3}$?

(a) $\dfrac{7}{20}$ (b) $\dfrac{6}{18}$

(c) $\dfrac{9}{27}$ (d) $\dfrac{17}{51}$

7. Choose the correct sign, which suits the below options.

(i) $\dfrac{3}{10}\ \square\ \dfrac{2}{5}$ (ii) $\dfrac{7}{5}\ \square\ \dfrac{11}{9}$

(a) >, < (b) >, > (c) <, < (d) <, >

8. Which of the following options represents the correct relation between A and B ?

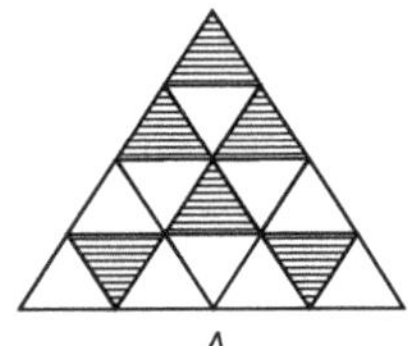
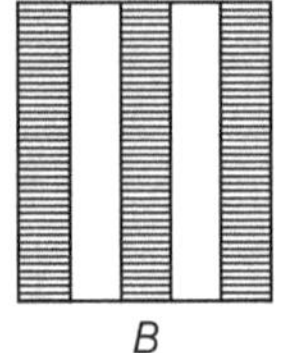

A   B

(a) $A > B$ (b) $A < B$ (c) $A = B$ (d) $A = \dfrac{B}{2}$

9. Arrange the given fractions in descending order.

$$\frac{4}{5},\ \frac{2}{3},\ \frac{4}{7},\ \frac{3}{5}$$

(a) $\dfrac{4}{7} > \dfrac{3}{5} > \dfrac{4}{5} > \dfrac{2}{3}$

(b) $\dfrac{2}{3} > \dfrac{4}{5} > \dfrac{4}{7} > \dfrac{3}{5}$

(c) $\dfrac{4}{5} > \dfrac{2}{3} > \dfrac{4}{7} > \dfrac{3}{5}$

(d) $\dfrac{4}{5} > \dfrac{2}{3} > \dfrac{3}{5} > \dfrac{4}{7}$

10. Match the following Column A to Column B.

Column A	Column B
I. $-\dfrac{5}{3} - \dfrac{1}{3}$	(i) $1\dfrac{1}{18}$
II. $1\dfrac{2}{9} - \dfrac{1}{6}$	(ii) $5\dfrac{2}{3}$
III. $\dfrac{17}{3}$	(iii) -2
IV. $9\dfrac{3}{7} + 4\dfrac{2}{7}$	(iv) $13\dfrac{5}{7}$

Codes

	I	II	III	IV
(a)	(ii)	(iv)	(i)	(iii)
(b)	(i)	(ii)	(iii)	(iv)
(c)	(iii)	(i)	(ii)	(iv)
(d)	(iv)	(ii)	(i)	(iii)

11. How many fifths are there in $3\dfrac{1}{5} + 4\dfrac{3}{5}$?

(a) $6\dfrac{3}{5}$ (b) $7\dfrac{4}{5}$

(c) $8\dfrac{2}{5}$ (d) $9\dfrac{1}{5}$

12. Find the sum of the shaded parts of the given figures I and II.

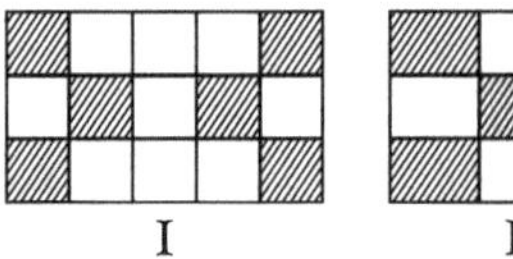

I   II

(a) $\dfrac{4}{15}$ (b) $\dfrac{23}{15}$

(c) $\dfrac{41}{45}$ (d) None of these

13. Which number should come in place of x?

$$\frac{4}{9} + \frac{7}{9} + \frac{x}{9} = 2\frac{1}{9}$$

(a) 7   (b) 1

(c) 8   (d) None of these

14. Suvidha is writing a test to give to her Mathematics class. She wants the test to include 40 multiple choice questions and 60 short answer questions. She has written 25 of the multiple choice questions. What fraction of the total test has she written?

(a) $\dfrac{1}{4}$ (b) $\dfrac{5}{8}$

(c) $\dfrac{2}{3}$ (d) $\dfrac{5}{12}$

15. Surbhi divided a chocolate pie into 17 parts. Her friend ate 5 out of them and she ate 3 out of them. Then, the fraction of chocolate pie remained is equal to

(a) $\dfrac{7}{17}$ (b) $\dfrac{8}{17}$

(c) $\dfrac{9}{17}$ (d) $\dfrac{10}{17}$

16. Meenakshi served $\dfrac{1}{4}$ of a dish to each guest at her party. If she expects 32 guests, then how much of such dish will she need?

(a) 6   (b) 8

(c) 32   (d) 128

17. Bhavna uses $\dfrac{3}{12}$ of her salary in transport, $\dfrac{4}{12}$ in shopping and rest in miscellaneous expenses? What fraction of the salary is used in miscellaneous expenses?

(a) $\dfrac{2}{12}$ (b) $\dfrac{3}{12}$

(c) $\dfrac{5}{12}$ (d) None of these

18. Sapna bought two oranges having 10 pieces in each one. She distributed it among 6 people equally including herself. What fraction of pieces does each one got?

(a) $1\dfrac{1}{3}$ (b) $3\dfrac{1}{3}$

(c) 3   (d) $\dfrac{5}{6}$

19. Vandana has worked $6\dfrac{5}{8}$ h of her regular 12 h day. How many more hours must she work?

(a) $5\dfrac{3}{8}$ (b) $\dfrac{23}{8}$

(c) $2\dfrac{1}{8}$ (d) None of these

20. A coffee container is $\dfrac{3}{5}$ full of beans. These beans are then put into another container having volume thrice that of the first one. What fraction of the large box is filled with beans?

(a) $\dfrac{2}{5}$ (b) $\dfrac{1}{5}$ (c) $\dfrac{3}{5}$ (d) 1

21. Daniel needs to make 16 flags for a school play. If he used $\dfrac{2}{5}$ of material to make these flags, then how many flags will be made, if he uses the remaining material as well?

(a) 16   (b) 20

(c) 24   (d) 27

22. Kanika is buying fabric for new curtains. There are three windows, each 35 inches wide. Kanika needs to buy fabric equal to $3\dfrac{1}{2}$ times the total width of the windows. How much fabric should she buy?

(a) $\dfrac{735}{2}$ inches   (b) 70 inches

(c) $312\dfrac{1}{2}$ inches   (d) None of these

2 Marks Questions

23. For a new year party, a caterer provided 3 kg of desserts. At the end of the party, there were $\frac{3}{5}$ kg of chocolate pudding, $\frac{4}{7}$ kg of caramel pudding and $\frac{5}{8}$ kg of fruit pudding left. What fraction of the original 3 kg was left after the parts?

(a) $1\frac{123}{280}$ (b) $1\frac{223}{280}$

(c) $1\frac{283}{270}$ (d) $1\frac{393}{290}$

24. In an activity class, students were asked to make a circular rangoli. Saria, Mehak, Chetna and Kanika made rangolies having different diameters as $\frac{17}{20}$ inches, $\frac{3}{4}$ inches, $\frac{5}{6}$ inches and $\frac{7}{10}$ inches, respectively. Who among them made the smallest one?

(a) Saria   (b) Mehak

(c) Chetna   (d) Kanika

25. If $A @ B = \dfrac{A+B}{A \times B}$, the value of $\dfrac{12@8}{8@4} + \dfrac{10@6}{6@2}$ is

(a) $\dfrac{41}{45}$ (b) $\dfrac{28}{31}$

(c) $\dfrac{43}{45}$ (d) $\dfrac{6}{19}$

26. If the weight of 5 packets of sugar is $155\frac{1}{5}$ g, $146\frac{1}{3}$ g, $161\frac{1}{2}$ g, $150\frac{1}{4}$ g and $148\frac{1}{6}$ g, then find

(i) The total weights of all the packets.

(ii) The difference between the weights of the heaviest packet and the lightest packet.

	(i)	(ii)
(a)	$\dfrac{15229}{20}$ g	$\dfrac{19}{16}$ g
(b)	$\dfrac{15229}{20}$ g	$\dfrac{91}{6}$ g
(c)	$\dfrac{25389}{20}$ g	$\dfrac{991}{6}$ g
(d)	$\dfrac{25389}{20}$ g	$\dfrac{911}{6}$ g

27. The length of Crayon Y is exactly half of the lengths of Crayon X and Crayon Z. What is the total length of Crayons X, Y and Z ?

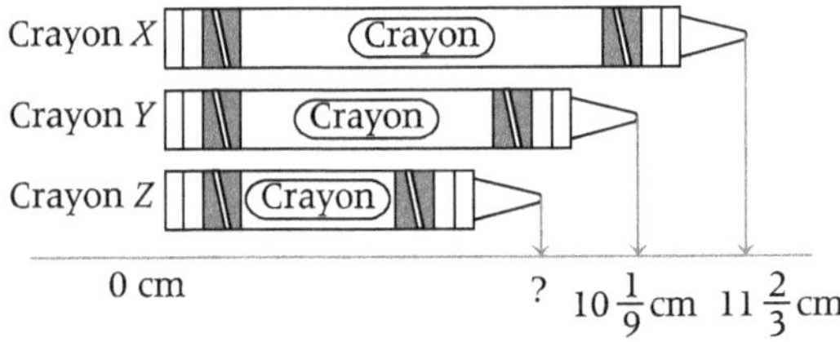

(a) $9\frac{1}{6}$ cm   (b) $30\frac{1}{3}$ cm

(c) $16\frac{1}{9}$ cm   (d) $28\frac{2}{9}$ cm

Decimals

1 Mark Questions

1. What is seven and five hundredths written as a decimal?

(a) 7.05 (b) 7.005

(c) 0.075 (d) 0.75

2. How is the decimal 90.9 written in words?

(a) Ninety nine

(b) Nine and nine hundredths

(c) Ninety and nine tenths

(d) Nine tenths and nine hundredths

3. The greatest possible decimal fraction upto four decimal places is

(a) 0.9900

(b) 0.0009

(c) 0.9999

(d) 0.9000

4. Which of the figures has a shaded part equal to 0.25?

(a) 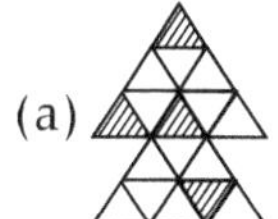

(b) 

(c) 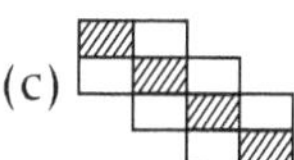

(d) None of the above

5. Which of the following number line represents the point $y = \dfrac{126}{630}$?

(a) 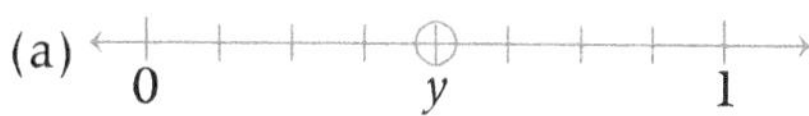

(b) 

(c) 

(d) 

6. Find the sum of all the decimal numbers represented by the point P, Q and R on the given number line.

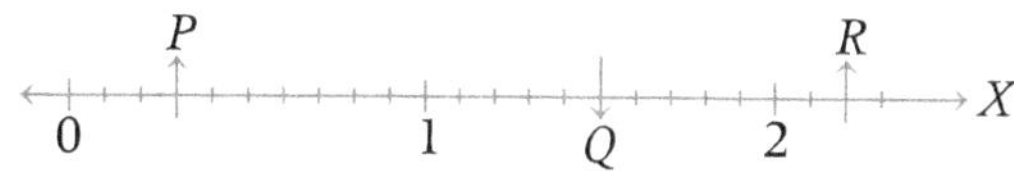

(a) 3.8

(b) 5.2

(c) 4

(d) 4.2

7. Which of the following decimals are arranged in ascending order?
   (a) 0.05, 0.06, 0.13, 0.01
   (b) 0.9, 0.4, 0.5, 0.2
   (c) 0.4, 0.09, 0.02, 0.01
   (d) 0.13, 0.16, 0.25, 0.5

8. Choose the correct option.
   (a) $56\% < 0.5$
   (b) $0.33 = \dfrac{4}{9}$
   (c) $36 > \dfrac{9}{25}$
   (d) $\dfrac{1}{7} > 0.186$

9. State 'T' for true and 'F' for false.
   I. 3 hundredths + 3 tenths = 33
   II. The place value of a digit at the tenths place is $\dfrac{1}{10}$ times the same digit at the hundredths place.
   III. $17.22 < 17.099$
   IV. The value of 10 coins of 40 paise is ₹ 40.

   Codes

	I	II	III	IV
(a)	F	T	F	T
(b)	T	F	T	F
(c)	T	T	T	T
(d)	F	F	F	F

10. The equivalent form of 7.24 is
    (a) $\dfrac{724}{10}$
    (b) $\dfrac{724}{90}$
    (c) $7\dfrac{6}{25}$
    (d) $8\dfrac{4}{90}$

11. Expanded form of 273.04 is
    (a) $200 + 70 + 3 + 0 + \dfrac{4}{10}$
    (b) $200 + 70 + 3 + \dfrac{0}{10} + \dfrac{4}{100}$
    (c) $20 + 7 + 3 + 0 + 4$
    (d) $200 + 70 + 30 + 0 + \dfrac{4}{10}$

12. If 0.090909 is approximately equal to $\dfrac{1}{11}$, then approximate value of 0.454545 is equal to
    (a) $\dfrac{4}{11}$
    (b) $\dfrac{5}{11}$
    (c) $\dfrac{45}{11}$
    (d) $\dfrac{4.5}{11}$

13. A bottle of orange juice is 1.5 liters and a bottle of apple juice is 1.35 liters. How many total liters of juice is in the two bottles?
    (a) 2.35 liters
    (b) 2.50 liters
    (c) 2.85 liters
    (d) 2.90 liters

14. The product of $7.2 \times 9.69 \times 0.0 \times 4.2$ is
    (a) 0.4762
    (b) 63.4246
    (c) 0
    (d) 1

2 Marks Questions

15. What will be the value of

$$\frac{(8.5 + 7.8 \times 6.5 \div 1.3 - 1)}{(7.5 \times 1.6 + 7.5 \times 0.4)}$$

(a) 4.2   (b) 3.1   (c) 9.86   (d) 6.75

16. Fill in the blanks with the help of options, given below:

(i) 14.57   (ii) 14.4   (iii) 0.865

(iv) 79.9   (v) 0.863   (vi) 14.6

(vii) 14.2   (viii) 79.009

  I. 0.8625 lies between 0.86 and ____.

  II. The fraction $14\dfrac{2}{10}$ is equal to ____.

  III. 14.572 correct to the tenths place is ____.

  IV. The value of 79 kg 9 gm is equal to ____ kg.

Codes

	I	II	III	IV
(a)	(v)	(vii)	(vi)	(viii)
(b)	(iii)	(ii)	(vi)	(viii)
(c)	(v)	(ii)	(iii)	(iv)
(d)	(iii)	(vii)	(ii)	(iv)

17. Arranging the following decimal numbers in descending order.

9.009, 0.99, 1.11, 0.09, 0.909, 10.101

(a) $0.09 > 0.909 > 0.99 > 9.009 > 1.11 > 10.101$

(b) $9.009 > 10.101 > 1.11 > 0.99 > 0.09 > 0.909$

(c) $1.11 > 10.101 > 9.009 > 0.909 > 0.99 > 0.09$

(d) $10.101 > 9.009 > 1.11 > 0.99 > 0.909 > 0.09$

18. The cost of two toys, three pencils and five rubbers is ₹ 234 and 50 p. What will be the cost of one rubber if the cost of two toys and three pencils is ₹ 210 ?

(a) ₹ 4.70   (b) ₹ 4.90

(c) ₹ 3.90   (d) ₹ 2.70

19. If $96.2205 = 9 \times A + 6 \times B + 2 \times C + \dfrac{2}{D} + 5 \times E,$

then the value of $4A + 5B + 2C + D + \dfrac{7}{E}$ is

(a) 45.7012   (b) 70145.2

(c) 14570.2   (d) 701.452

Ratio and Proportion

1 Mark Questions

1. Pick the odd one out.

(a) $9:12$ (b) $14:10$ (c) $28:20$ (d) $21:15$

2. If $a:b=2:3$ and $b:c=5:7$, then $a:b:c$ is equal to

(a) $6:10:14$ (b) $2:3:7$

(c) $10:15:21$ (d) None of these

3. The ratio of $\left(\dfrac{1}{4}\text{ of }12.40\right)$ to $(0.8\text{ of }1.35)$ is

(a) $\dfrac{31}{108}$ (b) $\dfrac{155}{54}$

(c) $\dfrac{48.6}{108}$ (d) None of these

4. A school played 30 cricket matches out of which they won 12 matches. What is the ratio of the number of matches played to the number of matches lost?

(a) $5:3$ (b) $3:5$ (c) $8:7$ (d) $7:8$

5. Find the ratio of shaded part to the unshaded part.

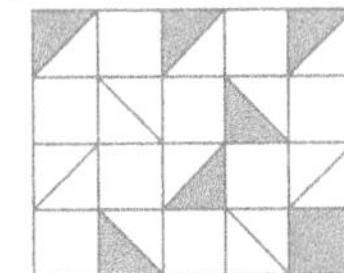

(a) $\dfrac{4}{12}$ (b) $\dfrac{1}{4}$

(c) $\dfrac{5}{16}$ (d) None of these

6. When x is added to both terms of the ratio $2:5$, it becomes $5:6$, then the value of x is

(a) 10   (b) 12

(c) 13   (d) None of these

7. If $\dfrac{4}{15}x=\dfrac{2}{5}y$, then ratio of $\dfrac{x+y}{x-y}$ is

(a) $\dfrac{3}{5}$ (b) 5   (c) $\dfrac{2}{5}$ (d) 3

8. The school start at $7:30$ am and is over at $1:00$ pm. If there are two breaks of 15 min and 25 min respectively, then find the ratio of the break time to the total time the students spend at school.

(a) $22:3$ (b) $3:22$ (c) $4:33$ (d) $33:4$

9. If $64:32=8:x$, then the value of x is

(a) 2   (b) 4   (c) 8   (d) 16

10. Mean proportional between a and b is

(a) $a+b$ (b) $\dfrac{a}{b}$ (c) ab (d) $\sqrt{ab}$

11. Fourth proportional to 3, 5, 18 is

(a) 15   (b) 30   (c) 27   (d) 35

12. What is the sum of the mean and third proportion, if 8, 16 and 32 are in the continued proportion?

(a) 42   (b) 24

(c) 48   (d) 12

13. If 5 tickets for a play cost ₹ 60, then the cost of 12 such tickets is

(a) ₹ 100 (b) ₹ 720 (c) ₹ 360 (d) ₹ 144

14. Gaika earned ₹ 24000/ month. She spent $\frac{2}{5}$ of it on the rent and ₹ 3600 on food. What is the ratio of his expense on the food to that of rent?

(a) 3 : 8 (b) 11 : 20 (c) 7 : 9 (d) 8 : 3

15. 14 men can do a piece of work in 24 days. How many men will be required if the work is to be complete in 16 days?

(a) 21 (b) 27 (c) 28 (d) 6

16. The ratio of the length to the breadth of a rectangle is 7 : 6. The semi-perimeter is 117 cm. What is the area of the rectangle?

(a) 420 sq units (b) 378 sq units

(c) 4914 sq units (d) None of these

17. Komal is 40 cm taller than Lipika. If their height is in the ratio 7 : 5, then find the height of Komal.

(a) 140 cm (b) 200 cm

(c) 100 cm (d) 120 cm

18. A shopkeeper has money to buy 50 items costing ₹ 525 each. If cost of each item increases by ₹ 100, the number of items he can buy is

(a) 40

(b) 45

(c) 42

(d) Can't be determined

19. Raghav, Vandana and Eva are given ₹ 520. They decide to divide the money in the ratio of their ages, 10 : 9 : 7. How much money does Vandana got?

(a) ₹ 200 (b) ₹ 180 (c) ₹ 140 (d) ₹ 270

2 Marks Questions

20. The ratio of the number of boys to the number of girls in an auditorium was 6 : 7. If $\frac{2}{3}$ of the boys left the auditorium, there would be 70 more girls than boys in the auditorium. How many students were in the auditorium at first?

(a) 26

(b) 91

(c) 176

(d) 182

21. Manoj gives ₹ 72000 as donation to an old age home and an orphanage in the ratio 5 : 4. Find the difference between the amount of money he gives to the an old age home and the orphanage.

(a) ₹ 10000

(b) ₹ 5000

(c) ₹ 4000

(d) ₹ 8000

22. If ₹ 1190 be divided among A, B and C in such a way that A gets $\frac{2}{3}$ of what B gets and B gets $\frac{1}{4}$ of what C gets, then their shares are respectively

(a) ₹ 210, ₹ 140, ₹ 960 (b) ₹ 840, ₹ 140, ₹ 260

(c) ₹ 140, ₹ 210, ₹ 840 (d) None of these

23. If length and breadth of a rectangular field is in the ratio 5 : 2, then find the value of

$$\frac{F + D - E + B - C}{A - D}$$

Length	20 cm	A	B
Breadth	C	12 cm	D
Perimeter	E	F	70 cm

(a) 2.75 (b) 3.5

(c) 4.6 (d) 6.25

Chapter

07

Algebra

1 Mark Questions

1. Choose the correct statement.
   (a) In $4x + 3 = 10$, x is the constant.
   (b) In $7y + 2 = 9z$, 2 is the variable.
   (c) Both (a) and (b)
   (d) None of the above

2. Which of the following are equations with a variable?

   A $\boxed{7 \times 6 - 3 = 39}$ B $\boxed{2x + 5 = 6}$

   C $\boxed{2 + 4 = 6}$ D $\boxed{3y - 5 = 16}$

   (a) Only A   (b) Only B
   (c) Only C   (d) Both B and D

3. In the simplified value of
   $4u + 13t - 10u + 5t$, coefficient of u is
   (a) $+6$ (b) -6
   (c) -14 (d) $+14$

4. If $14\left(\dfrac{a}{2} - 2\right) + 4 = \dfrac{4}{a} + 9$, find the degree of the equation.
   (a) 1   (b) 2
   (c) 3   (d) None of these

5. Twelve less that 3 times a number is 27. What is the number?
   (a) 13   (b) 9   (c) 6   (d) 3

6. The value of $\dfrac{7y - 2}{5}$, when $y = 6$, is equal to
   (a) $\dfrac{11}{5}$ (b) $\dfrac{12}{5}$
   (c) 15   (d) 8

7. Which ratio best expresses the statement, 10 h is what percent of a day?
   (a) $\dfrac{10}{100} = \dfrac{x}{24}$
   (b) $\dfrac{10}{24} = \dfrac{x}{100}$
   (c) Both (a) and (b)
   (d) None of the above

8. Prerna bought 7 times the number of t-shirts as the number of jeans. Which of the following cannot be the total number of clothes she bought?
   (a) 24   (b) 40
   (c) 46   (d) 56

9. Andrew weighs $(x + 3)$ kg. Catherin weighs 2 kg less than Andrew. Bendrick weighs 1 kg more than Catherin. What is the total mass of the three?
   (a) $(3x + 2)$ kg
   (b) $(x + 3)$ kg
   (c) $(3x + 6)$ kg
   (d) $(2x + 6)$ kg

10. Monika is now $24\,p$ yr old. She is thrice as old as Ben. What was their total age 4 yr ago?

(a) $(30p - 4)$ yr   (b) $(32p - 8)$ yr

(c) $(30p + 4)$ yr   (d) $(24p - 8)$ yr

11. The algebraic expression for the statement, "Product of x and reciprocal of a subtracted from product of y and reciprocal of b" is

(a) $-\left(\dfrac{x}{a} - \dfrac{y}{b}\right)$ (b) $-\left(\dfrac{x - y}{a - b}\right)$

(c) $xa - yb$ (d) $\dfrac{1}{xa - yb}$

12. Which equation is equivalent to
$$5x - 2(7x + 1) = 14x$$

(a) $-9x - 2 = 14x$ (b) $-9x + 1 = 14x$

(c) $-9x + 2 = 14x$ (d) $12x - 1 = 14x$

13. Simplify and choose the correct option.
$$7x - [3y - \{4x - (5z - 3y) + 6z$$
$$- 3(2x + y - 3z)\}]$$

(a) $7x - 4y + 11z$ (b) $8x + 3y - 10z$

(c) $5x - 3y + 10z$ (d) None of these

14. If $\dfrac{3}{4}P - 3\dfrac{1}{3} = 4\dfrac{1}{3}$, then value of P is

(a) 46   (b) 72

(c) 81   (d) None of these

15. Which of the following best describes the sum of the three numbers multiplied by the sum of their reciprocals?

(a) $(x + y + z) \times \left(\dfrac{1}{x + y + z}\right)$

(b) $(x + y + z) \times \left(\dfrac{1}{x} + \dfrac{1}{y} + \dfrac{1}{z}\right)$

(c) $(xyz) \times \left(\dfrac{1}{x + y + z}\right)$

(d) $(x + y + z) \times \left(\dfrac{1}{xyz}\right)$

16. Ashton divided ₹ x equally among her 2 sons and a daughter. Her daughter spent her money on 3 books that costs ₹ 30 each. How much money did her daughter have left?

(a) ₹ $\left(\dfrac{x}{3} - 4\right)$ (b) ₹ $\left(\dfrac{x - 25}{3}\right)$

(c) ₹ $\left(\dfrac{x}{3} - 90\right)$ (d) ₹ $\left(\dfrac{x}{4} - 25\right)$

17. The length of the smallest side of a triangle is 5 units less than the other side while the length of the largest side is 2 more than twice its other side. Write the expression to represent the perimeter of the triangle.

(a) $4x - 3$ units   (b) $2x - 5$ units

(c) $4x - 8$ units   (d) $2x + 5$ units

18. The total cost in rupees of renting a cycle for n days is given by the equation $C = 120 + 20n$.

If the total cost was ₹ 360, for how many days was the cycle rented?

(a) 10   (b) 12

(c) 24   (d) 36

19. Sadhvi had blue and red pens in the ratio 2 : 3. If the sum of the numbers of pens is 25, then the numbers of blue and red pens, respectively are

(a) 20 and 30   (b) 12 and 13

(c) 10 and 15   (d) None of these

20. Fill in the blanks with the help of options, given below.

(i) $\dfrac{20}{r}$,   (ii) equation,

(iii) variable,   (iv) $5 + x + 9$,

(v) $5x + 9$,   (vi) 4,

(vii) $20r$

    I. 9 more than 5 times the number x can be represented as __________.

II. $x =$ _________ is a solution of the equation $7 - x = 3$.

III. An expression with a variable, constant and the sign of equality is called an _________.

IV. The time taken to cover a distance of 20 km at a speed of r km/h is _________.

Codes

	I	II	III	IV
(a)	(iv)	(vi)	(iii)	(vii)
(b)	(v)	(vii)	(iii)	(vii)
(c)	(iv)	(vii)	(ii)	(i)
(d)	(v)	(vi)	(ii)	(i)

2 Marks Questions

21. In the given rectangle $ABCD$, if length (AB) is increased by $3x$ and breadth (BC) is decreased by x, then find the new perimeter.

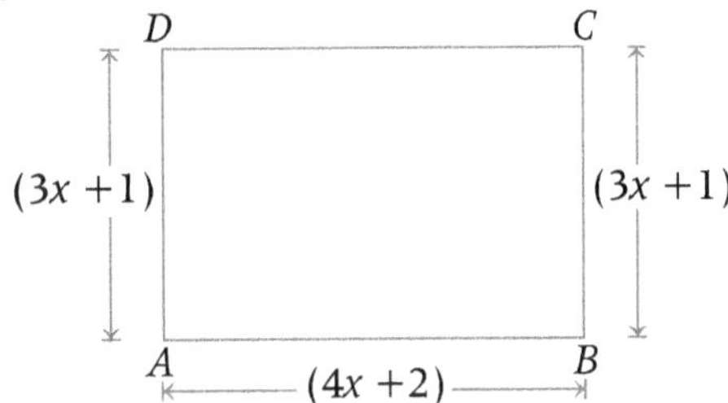

(a) $(18x + 6)$ units   (b) $(9x + 3)$ units

(c) $(5x + 6)$ units   (d) $(10x + 6)$ units

22. There were x females and half as many males as females at a restaurant in the morning. An hour later, twice the number of females and 60 males visited the restaurant. How many peoples were at the restaurant altogether?

(a) $4 + \dfrac{x}{2} + 60$ (b) $\dfrac{7x}{2} + 60$

(c) $4x + \dfrac{60x}{2}$ (d) $4 + 4x + \dfrac{1}{2}$

23. While solving a problem given below, Avinash made a mistake while writing the steps. Identify the wrong step.

Solve $6(2x + 3) - 3(3x - 2) = 30$

Step-1 Expand the brackets.

$$6 \times 2x + 6 \times 3 - 3 \times 3x \times + 3 \times 2 = 30$$
$$\Rightarrow \quad 12x + 18 - 9x + 6 = 30$$

Step-2 Combine the like terms.

$$(12x - 9x) + (18 + 6) = 30$$
$$\Rightarrow \quad 3x + 24 = 30$$

Step-3 Add 24 to both sides gives $3x = 6$

Step-4 Divide by 3 on both sides.

$$3x \div 3 = 6 \div 3$$
$$\Rightarrow \quad x = 2$$

(a) Only Step-1

(b) Only Step-2

(c) Only Step-3

(d) Only Step-4

24. Read the following statements carefully and select the correct option.

Statement-I If the sum of one-half, one-third and one-fourth of a number exceeds $\dfrac{3}{4}$th of the number by 30, then the number is 90.

Statement-II A number y is added with four times the number itself. If the result is subtracted from the greatest two-digit number, then the answer is $98 - 5y$.

(a) Statement-I is true but Statement-II is false.

(b) Statement-I is false but Statement-II is true.

(c) Both Statement-I and Statement-II are true.

(d) Both Statement-I and Statement-II are false.

Elementary Shapes

1 Mark Questions

1. Which of the following set of angles are acute, obtuse, right, straight, reflex respectively?
(a) 28°, 100°, 60°, 180°, 210°
(b) 100°, 28°, 90°, 180°, 120°
(c) 100°, 28°, 180°, 90°, 120°
(d) 28°, 100°, 90°, 180°, 210°

2. Which of the following represent reflex angle?

(a) 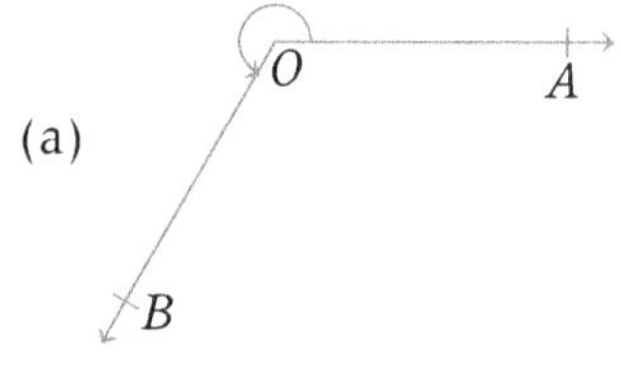

(b) 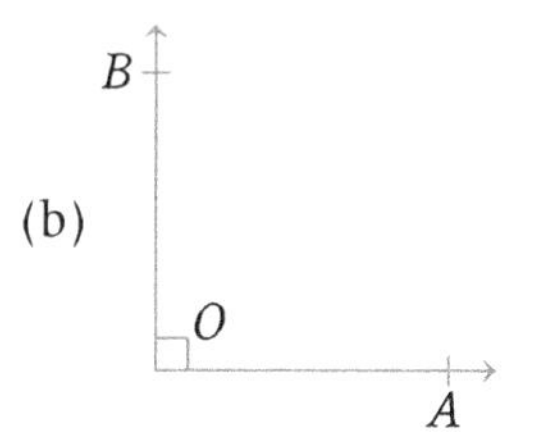

(c) 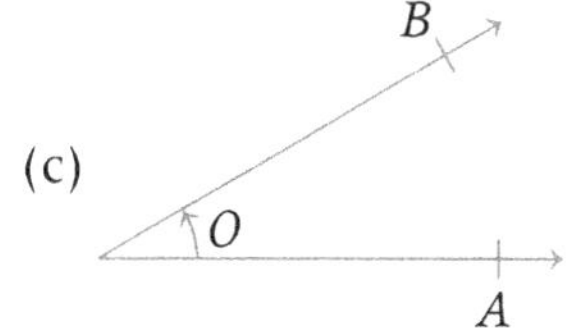

(d) 

3. The number of obtuse angles is

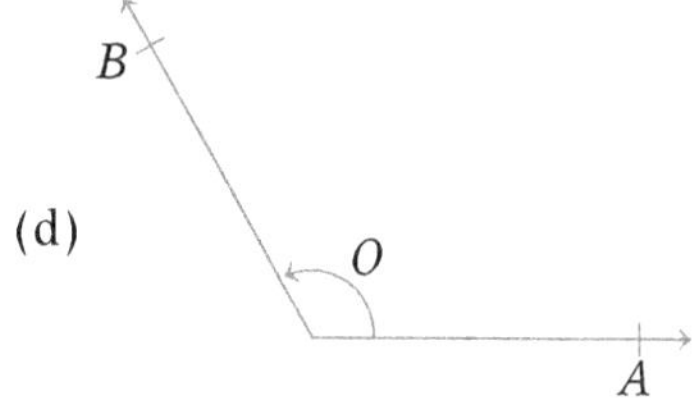

(a) 2   (b) 3
(c) 4   (d) 5

4. Choose the pair of supplementary angles from the options given below.
(a) 100° and 200°
(b) 115° and 65°
(c) 30° and 180°
(d) 60° and 90°

5. How many degrees are there in $2\frac{1}{3}$ right angles?
(a) 360°   (b) 210°   (c) 150°   (d) 108°

6. Find the supplement of an angle which is 4 times of its complement.
   (a) 150°   (b) 105°
   (c) 130°   (d) 60°

7. If a bicycle wheel has 50 spokes, then find the angle between a pair of two consecutive spokes.
   (a) $5\dfrac{1}{2}^{\circ}$ (b) $7\dfrac{1}{5}^{\circ}$
   (c) $\dfrac{2}{11}^{\circ}$ (d) $\dfrac{2}{15}^{\circ}$

8. Two supplementary angles are in the ratio of $4:5$. Find the angles.
   (a) 40° and 50°
   (b) 84° and 96°
   (c) 60° and 120°
   (d) 80° and 100°

9. Which one of the following is correct about the given triangle ?

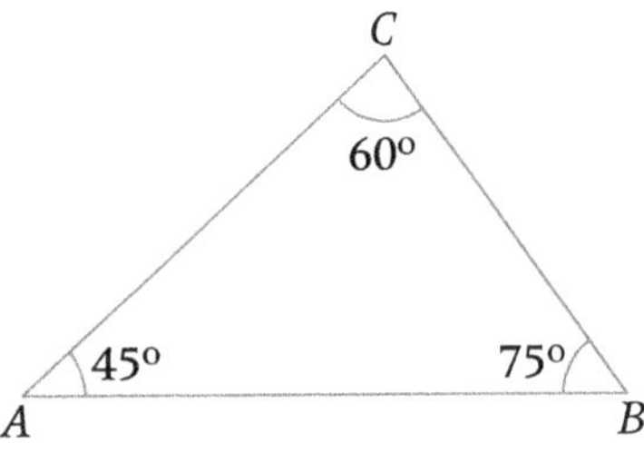

   (a) All angles are right angles.
   (b) All angles are acute angles.
   (c) The sum of the angles of the triangle is more than 180°.
   (d) Both (a) and (b)

10. A scalene triangle can .... be a right triangle.
    (a) Always
    (b) Never
    (c) Sometimes
    (d) Can't be determined

11. Match the columns.

Column I (Measurement of Triangle)	Column II (Type of Triangles)
A. Triangle which has three sides of equal length.	(p) Scalene
B. Triangle which has two sides of equal length.	(q) Equilateral
C. Triangle which has one right angle with two sides of equal length.	(r) Isosceles
D. Triangle which has all sides are of different length.	(s) Isosceles right angled

   (a) A → (r), B → (p), C → (s), D → (q)
   (b) A → (p), B → (r), C → (q), D → (s)
   (c) A → (q), B → (s), C → (r), D → (p)
   (d) A → (q), B → (r), C → (s), D → (p)

12. How many complete turns is equivalent to 180° ?
    (a) 2   (b) 1
    (c) $\dfrac{1}{2}$ (d) $\dfrac{1}{4}$

13. Find the measure of the smaller angle formed by the hour hand and the minute hand of a clock at 4' O clock.
    (a) 160°   (b) 240°   (c) 90°   (d) 120°

14. At $6:50$ what type of angle is formed between the two hands of a clock?
    (a) An obtuse angle
    (b) A right angle
    (c) An acute angle
    (d) A straight angle

15. How many right angles are there in the given figure?

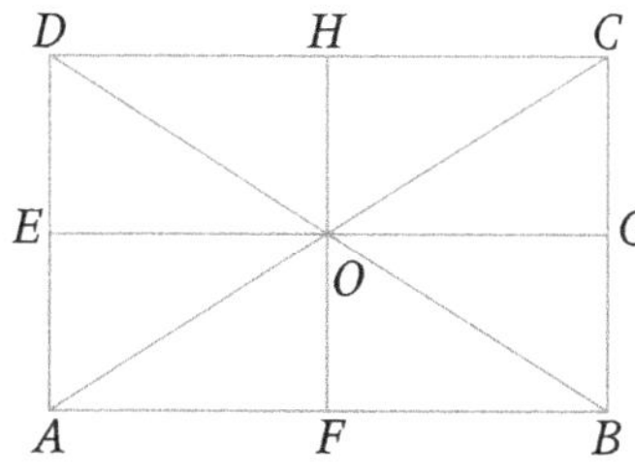

(a) 14   (b) 18

(c) 16   (d) 15

16. $ABCD$ is a quadrilateral. $AB = BC = CD = DA$ and $\angle A = \angle B = \angle C = \angle D = 90°$. Then $ABCD$ can be called ....

(a) Square

(b) Trapezium

(c) Kite

(d) Rectangle

17. Find the value of x and y from the figure of a parallelogram given below.

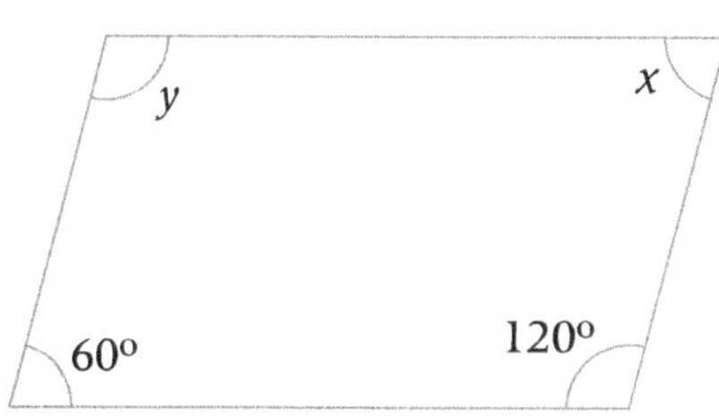

(a) $x = 90°$, $y = 130°$

(b) $y = 120°$, $x = 60°$

(c) $y = 130°$, $x = 60°$

(d) All of these

18. In the following figure find the value of y.

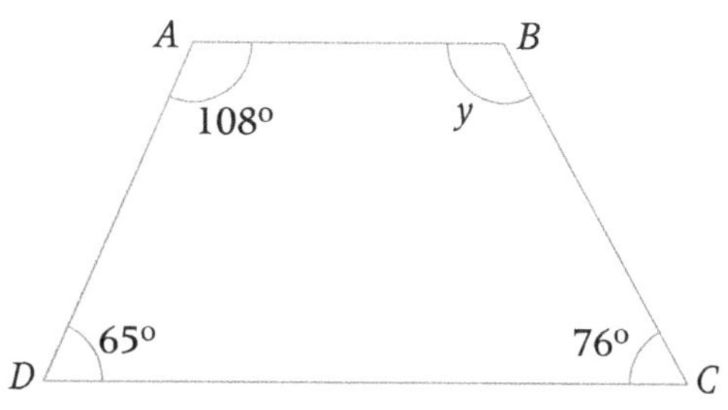

(a) 249°   (b) 111°   (c) 200°   (d) 105°

19. In the given figure, $ABCD$ is a quadrilateral. $\angle ADB = 60°$, $\angle BAC = 70°$, $\angle DBC = 30°$ and $\angle ACB = 60°$, find $\angle DAC$.

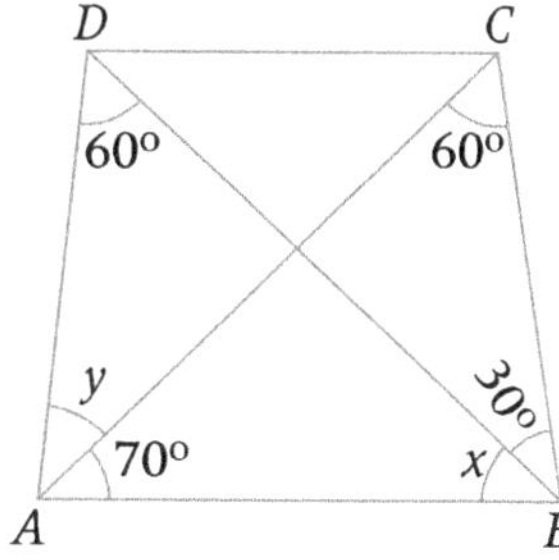

(a) 60°   (b) 50°

(c) 30°   (d) 20°

20. A cuboid with all the edges of same length is called a ....

(a) Cube   (b) Square

(c) Rhombus   (d) Kite

21. How many faces does a sphere has?

(a) 2   (b) 3

(c) 1   (d) 0

2 Marks Questions

22. Match the columns.

	Column I		Column II
A.	The term which is associated with an edge of your book is	(p)	A right triangle
B.	The angle formed at each corner of an envelope is	(q)	113°
C.	The angle formed by minute hand in 10 min is	(r)	A line segment
D.	The supplement of five-sixth of a right angle is	(s)	Right angle
E.	If one angle of a triangle is equal to the sum of the other two equal angles, then the triangle is	(t)	acute
F.	The difference between the supplement of an angle and the angle is 46°. The supplement is	(u)	105°

(a) A → (r), B → (t), C → (s), D → (p),
   E → (u), F → (q)
(b) A → (s), B → (t), C → (u), D → (p),
   E → (q), F → (r)
(c) A → (s), B → (q), C → (r), D → (p),
   E → (t), F → (u)
(d) A → (r), B → (s), C → (t), D → (u),
   E → (p), F → (q)

23. In the figure given below, find the values of $x + y - z$.

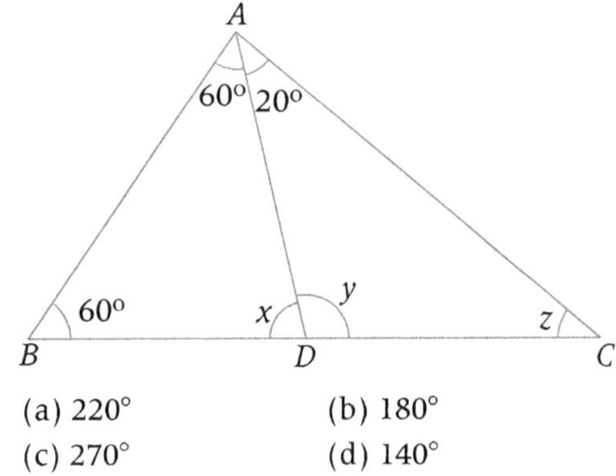

(a) 220°
(b) 180°
(c) 270°
(d) 140°

24. Find the value of $X + Y - Z$.

Shape	Faces	Vertices	Edges
Triangular Prism	5	X	9
Square Pyramid	5	5	Y
Pentagonal Prism	7	Z	15

(a) 8
(b) 4
(c) 5
(d) 7

Chapter 09

Geometry

1 Mark Questions

A. Lines and Angles

1. Which of the following statements is false?

(a) Using protractor, angle of any measure between 0° and 180° can be drawn.

(b) A line has two end points.

(c) An angle whose measure is greater than 90° is an obtuse angle.

(d) Two coinciding rays with a common end point form an angle of measure 0°.

2. There are four lines in a plane, no two of which are parallel. The maximum number of points in which they can intersect, is

(a) 7 (b) 5

(c) 6 (d) None of these

3. The minimum number of lines that must bind a plane figure is

(a) 4 (b) 3

(c) 2 (d) None of these

4. PQ of length 8.5 cm. From P, an arc of 6.2 cm is cut off. Find the length of RQ.

(a) 1.4 cm (b) 1.6 cm

(c) 2.3 cm (d) 1.8 cm

5. Given figure shows an angle of ......, if arc BD = arc DE.

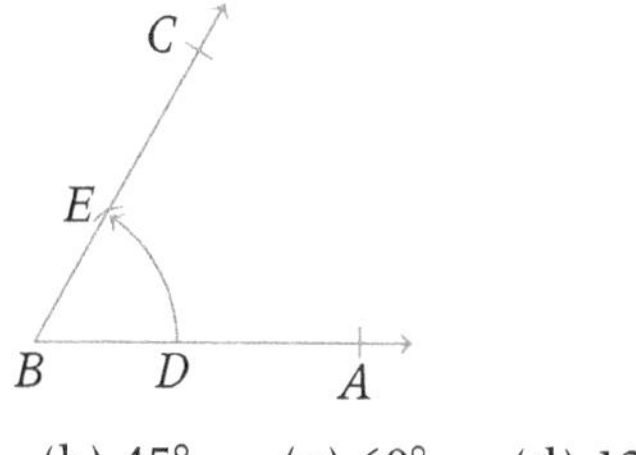

(a) 90° (b) 45° (c) 60° (d) 120°

6. The given diagram is in the shape of a semi-circle. Which of the following options shows a right angle?

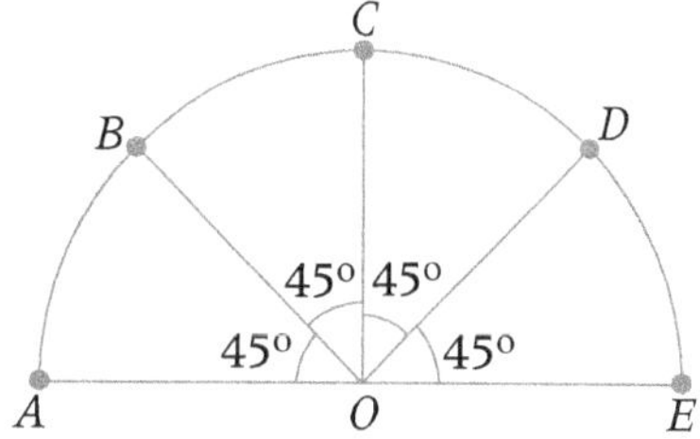

(a) ∠BOE (b) ∠BOA

(c) ∠AOE (d) ∠BOD

7. If a cart wheel makes six and a half turns, then the number of straight angles through which it turns, are

(a) 10 (b) 11

(c) 13 (d) 16

8. Given $\angle ABC = 60°$. If we divide it into five equal angles, then measure of each angle would be

(a) 20°   (b) 15°

(c) 12°   (d) 7.5°

B. Triangles and Circles

9. In the given figure below, $\angle ACB = 90°$ and $CD \perp AB$. The number of right angled triangles in the figure is

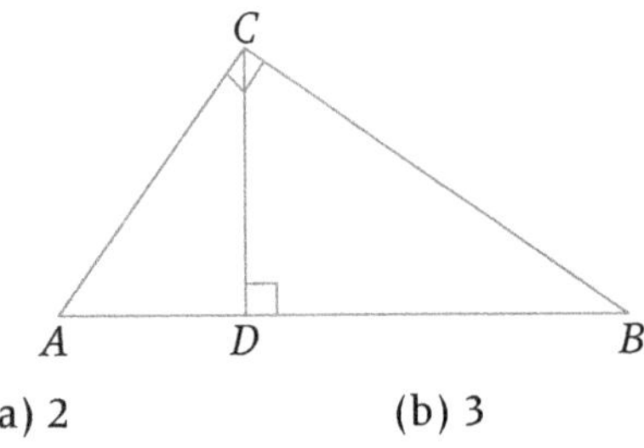

(a) 2   (b) 3

(c) 1   (d) 4

10. The number of triangles in the figure below is

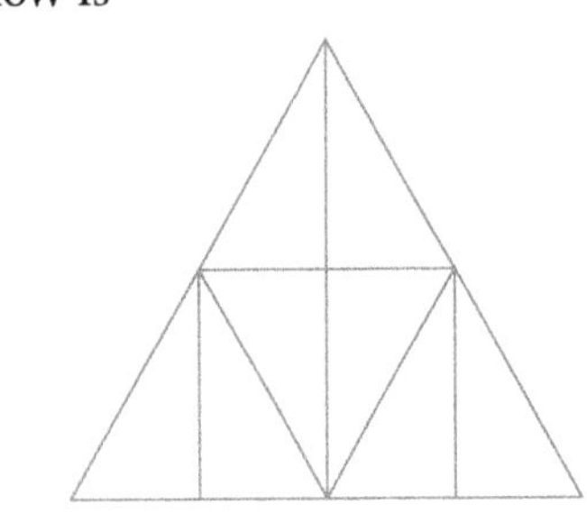

(a) 17   (b) 15

(c) 8   (d) 16

11. How many triangles can be made within a septagon?

(a) 4   (b) 5

(c) 6   (d) 7

12. In a ΔLMN, $LM \perp NM$, $LM = 4$ cm and $MN = 4$ cm, then ΔLMN is

(a) An isosceles right angled triangle.

(b) Isosceles but not a right angled triangle.

(c) A right angled triangle but not isosceles.

(d) Neither isosceles not right angled triangle.

13. State 'P' for possible and 'N' for not possible.

  I. A triangle with sides 2 cm, 1 cm and 4 cm can be drawn.

  II. A triangle can have two obtuse angles.

 III. A triangle can have all three acute angles.

 IV. A right angled triangles has all angles equal to 90°.

Codes

	I	II	III	IV			I	II	III	IV
(a)	P	N	P	N		(b)	N	N	P	N
(c)	P	P	P	N		(d)	N	P	N	P

14. A cow is tied with a rope of length 10 cm and allowed to graze around the field. Which of the shape can be formed by the part grazed by the cow?

(a) Quadrilateral of sides 10 cm

(b) Circle of radius 10 cm

(c) Triangle of sides 10 cm

(d) Quadrant of a circle of arc length 5 cm

15. Match the following:

List-I	List-II
A. Concentric circles have different radii but same	1. Set squares
B. Two lines which never intersect each other are called	2. Protractor
C. Semi-circular shaped instrument in the geometrical box is called	3. Centre
D. The triangular shaped instruments in the geometrical box are called	4. Parallel line

Codes

	A	B	C	D			A	B	C	D
(a)	1	3	4	2		(b)	2	3	1	4
(c)	3	4	2	1		(d)	4	1	2	3

C. Miscellaneous

16. Which of the following statement is true about the given figure?

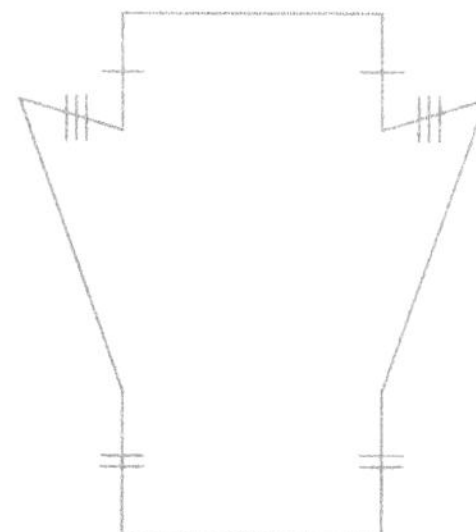

  (a) It is an octagon.

  (b) It is a regular polygon.

  (c) It is a polygon.

  (d) It is a quadrilateral.

17. If a quadrilateral has 2 diagonals, then a pentagon has __________ number of diagonals.

  (a) 3

  (b) 4

  (c) 5

  (d) 7

18. A polygon is drawn with prime number of sides such that the number lies between 5 and 10. If diagonals are to be drawn and counted, then which of the following will be equal to it?

  (a) 6

  (b) 12

  (c) 14

  (d) Can't be determined

19. State 'T' for true and 'F' for false.

  I. A single point has width.

  II. Infinite number of distinct lines can be drawn through two points.

  III. An octagon has 8 diagonals.

  IV. Every chord of circle divides it into two equal parts.

  Codes

	I	II	III	IV
(a)	F	T	F	T
(b)	T	T	T	T
(c)	F	F	F	F
(d)	T	F	T	F

20. A solid object when seen from bottom looks like

The same solid, when viewed from front looks like

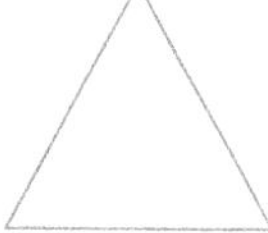

Which is the shape of the object?

(a) 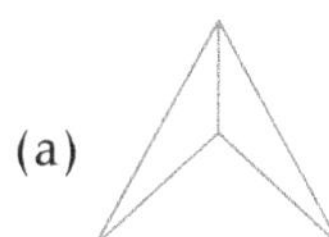   (b) 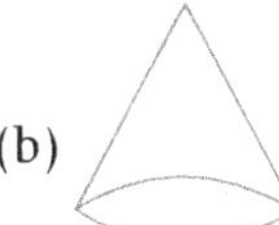

(c)    (d) 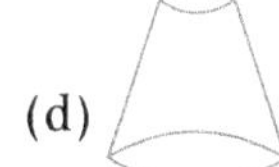

2 Marks Questions

21. Some cities are being connected in such a way that only 27 diagonal roads can be constructed between them and no three cities are collinear. Which of the following can be constructed, if the cities are connected by non-intersected lines?

(a) Hexagon

(b) Octagon

(c) Nonagon

(d) Can't be determined

22. What is the value of x in the following figure?

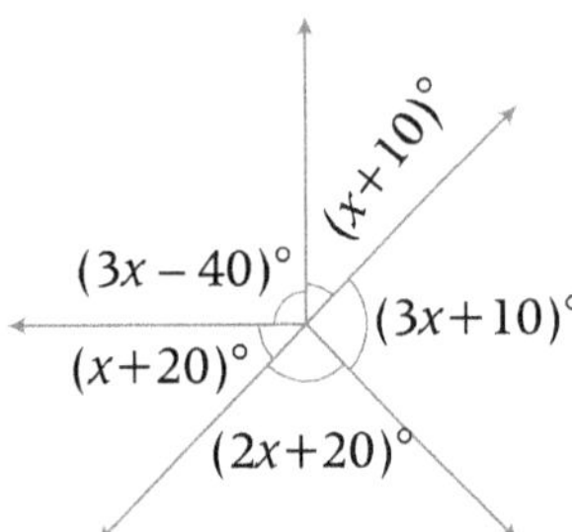

(a) 34°

(b) 26°

(c) 12°

(d) 17°

23. In the given figure, if O is the centre of the circle, then find the length of RS.

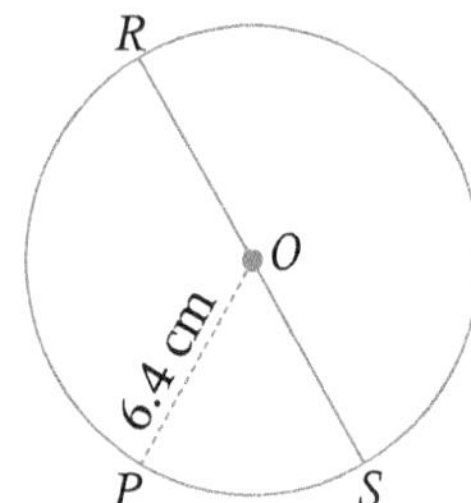

(a) 14.2 cm

(b) 16.4 cm

(c) 12.2 cm

(d) 12.8 cm

24. O is a point on the circle and P is a point in the exterior of the circle. Length of $\overline{OP} = 7.5$ cm and radius of the circle is 5.5 cm. What will be the length of $\overline{QP}$, if Q is the centre of the circle?

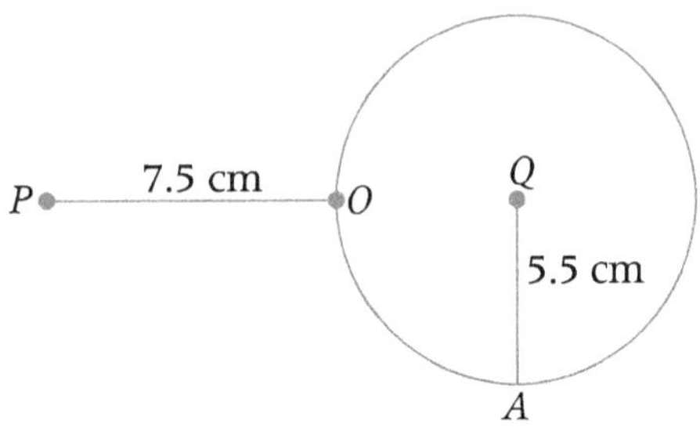

(a) 5.5 cm (b) 13 cm

(c) 7.5 cm (d) 13.5 cm

25. Fill in the blanks with the help of options, given below.

(i) straight, (ii) parallel,

(iii) initial, (iv) zero,

(v) intersecting, (vi) end point,

(vii) two, (viii) infinite

I. An angle 0° is called a __________ angle.

II. An angle with measure 180° is called a __________ angle.

III. The starting point of a ray is called the __________ point.

IV. __________ number of radii can be drawn in a circle.

V. If two lines have one common point, they are called __________ lines.

Codes

	I	II	III	IV	V
(a)	(i)	(iv)	(v)	(vii)	(ii)
(b)	(iv)	(i)	(iii)	(viii)	(v)
(c)	(i)	(iv)	(v)	(vi)	(ii)
(d)	(iv)	(i)	(iii)	(vi)	(iv)

Symmetry

Chapter 10

1 Mark Questions

1. Which of the following is not symmetrical about its diagonals?
   (a) Square
   (b) Rectangle
   (c) Rhombus
   (d) None of the above

2. How many lines of symmetry does the regular pentagon have?
   (a) 3 (b) 4
   (c) 5 (d) 2

3. The number of lines of symmetry in a protractor is
   (a) 0
   (b) 1
   (c) 2
   (d) More than 2

4. The number of lines of symmetry in a 30°-60°-90° set square is ....
   (a) 0 (b) 1
   (c) 2 (d) 3

5. How many minimum number of squares that must be added so that the line *MN* becomes a line of symmetry?

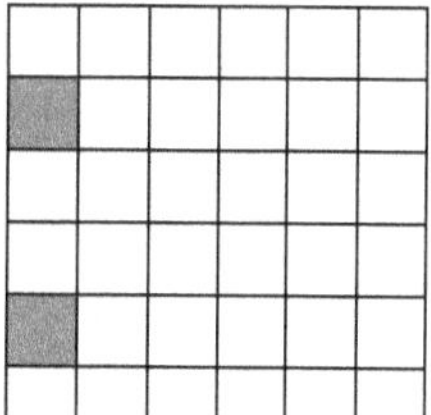

   (a) 4
   (b) 6
   (c) 3
   (d) 5

6. How many lines of symmetry does the given figure have?

   (a) 2 (b) 3
   (c) 4 (d) 1

7. The number of lines of symmetry in the given figure is ....

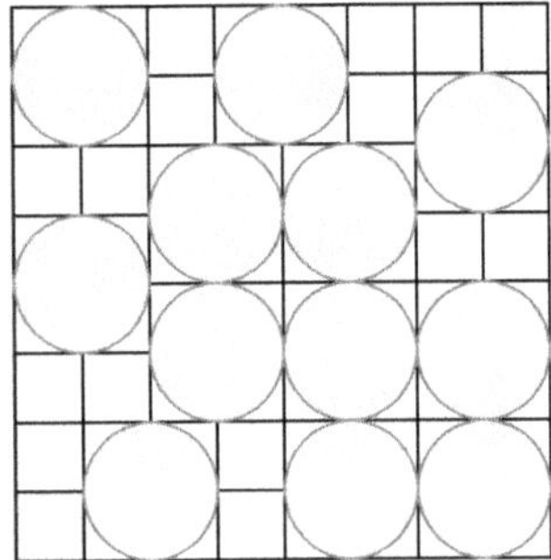

(a) 2   (b) 0
(c) 1   (d) 4

8. Which of the following figures has at least one line of symmetry?

P    Q 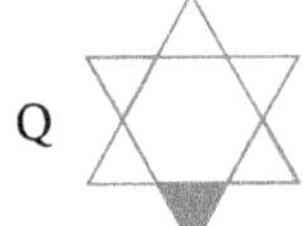

R 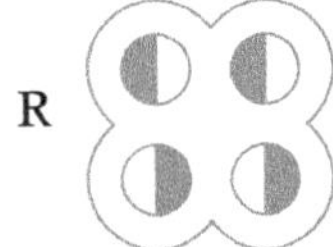   S 

(a) Only P   (b) Only P and S
(c) Only P, Q and S   (d) P, Q, R and S

9. Which of the following figures have at least two lines of symmetry?

P 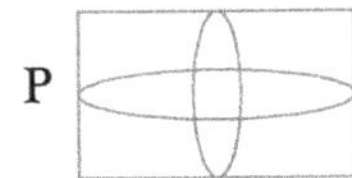   Q 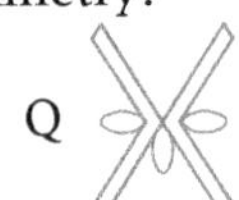

R    S

(a) Only Q and R   (b) Only P and S
(c) P, Q, R and S   (d) Only P and R

10. Which of the following figures has a line of symmetry?

(a) 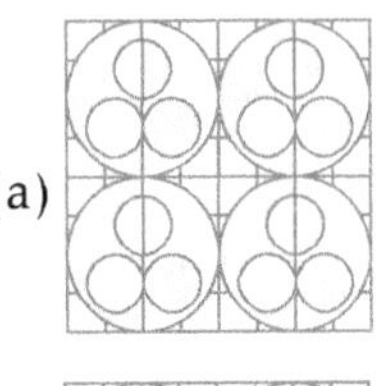   (b) 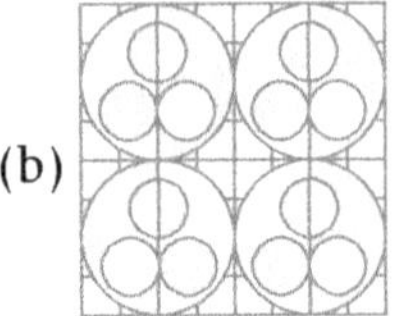

(c) 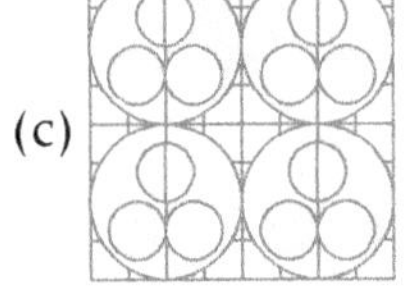   (d) 

11. Which of the following figures has exactly one lines of symmetry?

(a) 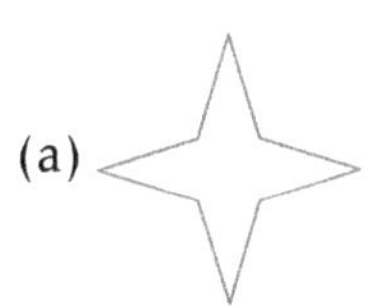   (b) 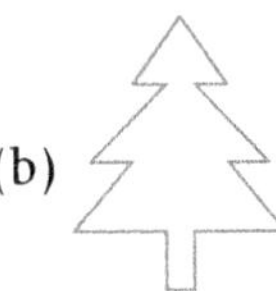

(c) 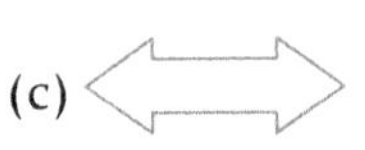   (d) 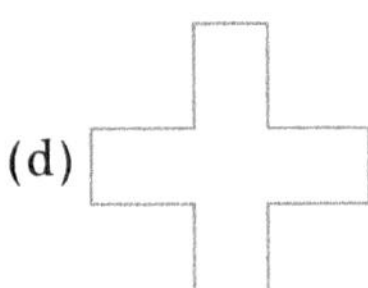

12. How many lines of symmetry does the following figures have?

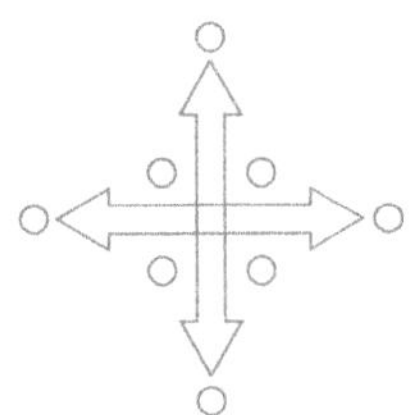   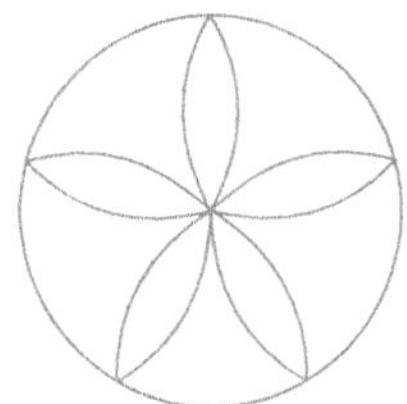

	(i)	(ii)
(a)	2	2
(b)	5	4
(c)	3	5
(d)	4	5

13. Which of the following alphabets has both horizontal and vertical line of symmetry?

(a) 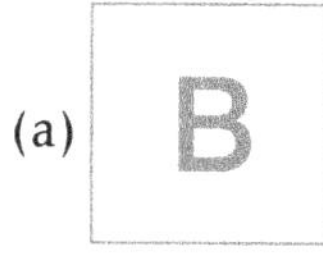

(b) 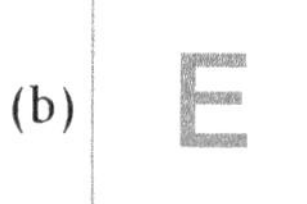

(c) 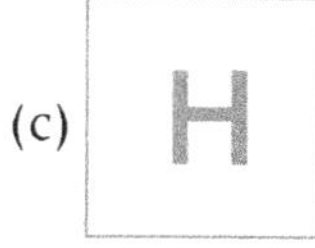

(d) All of these

14. Which of the following digits have exactly one line of symmetry?

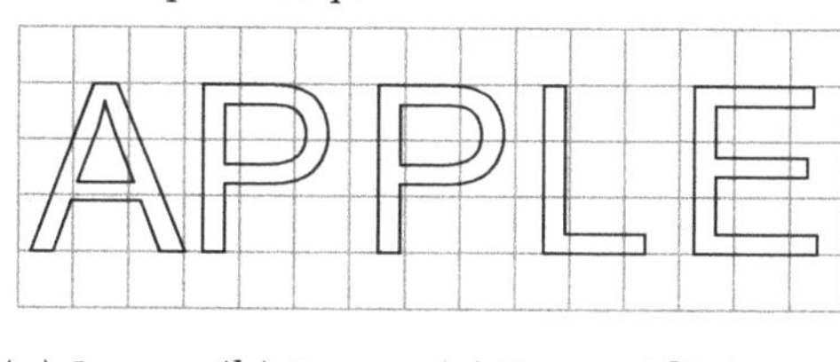

(a) 0   (b) 3   (c) 6   (d) 8

15. How many of the following letters have a line of symmetry?

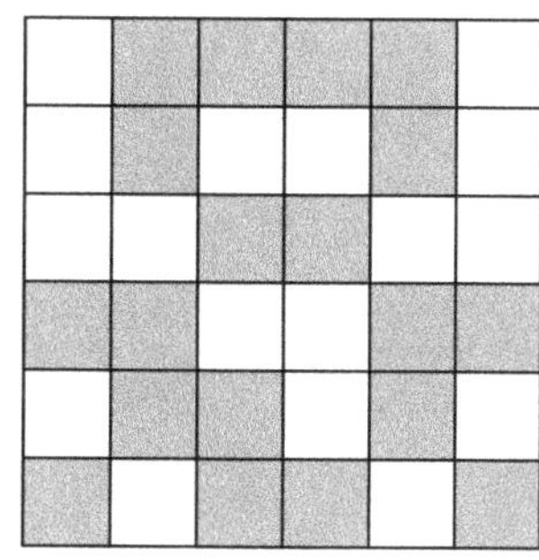

(a) 1   (b) 2   (c) 3   (d) 4

16. How many minimum number of squares must be shaded to make the given figure symmetrical?

(a) 1   (b) 2   (c) 3   (d) 4

17. What is the least number of squares that must be added so that the line *MN* becomes a line of symmetry?

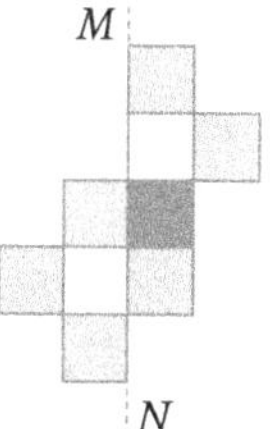

(a) 4   (b) 6
(c) 5   (d) 7

18. Complete the figure so that line *l* becomes the line of symmetry of the whole figure.

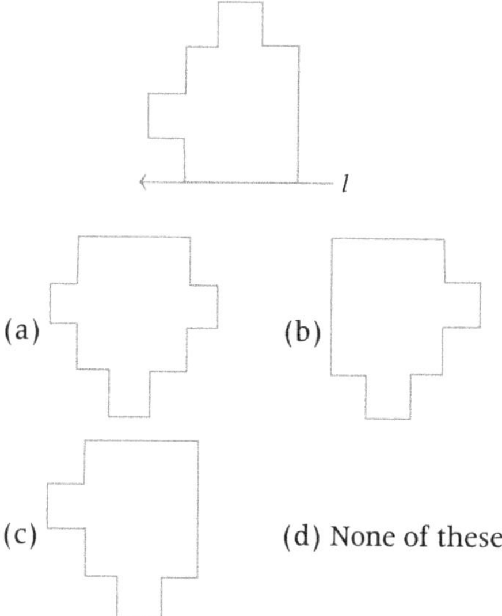

(a)   (b)

(c)   (d) None of these

19. Which of the following shapes is not symmetrical?

(a) 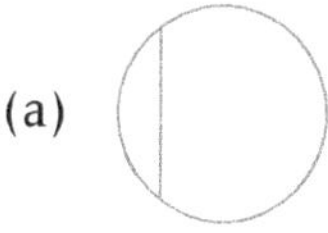   (b) 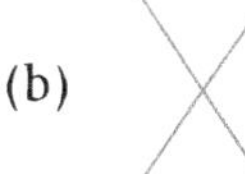

(c)    (d) 

20. Read the statements carefully and state 'T' for true and 'F' for false.

(i) Each diameter of a circle is an axis of symmetry.

(ii) A regular polygon has as many lines of symmetry as the number of sides.

(iii) Each one of the letters H, I, M, B of the English alphabet has atleast two lines of symmetry.

(iv) A line segment is symmetrical about its perpendicular bisector.

Codes

	(i)	(ii)	(iii)	(iv)
(a)	F	T	T	F
(b)	T	T	F	T
(c)	T	F	F	T
(d)	T	T	T	T

2 Marks Questions

21. Which of the following square(s) must be shaded so that given figure is symmetric along both the lines *XY* and *RS*?

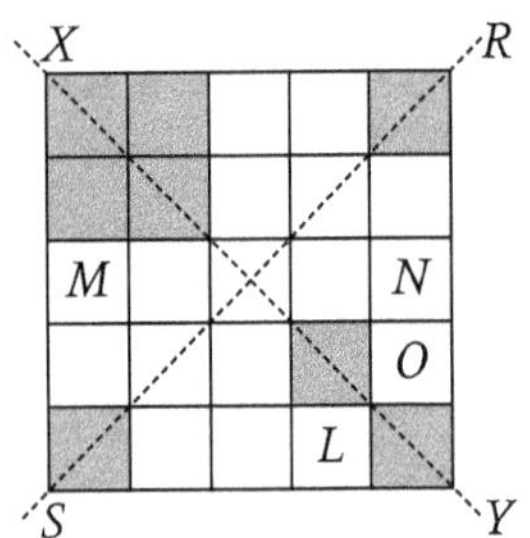

(a) *N* and *M*   (b) *O* only

(c) *L* and *O*   (d) *L* only

22. In ΔPQR, if $PQ = PR$, $QX \perp PR$, $RY \perp PQ$ and $PZ \perp QR$, then ΔPQR is symmetrical about ....

(a) *YR*

(b) *PZ*

(c) *QX*

(d) *PR*

23. Fill in the blanks and select the correct option.

(i) A rhombus has two lines of symmetry along its ....

(ii) All the lines of symmetry of the circle pass through its ....

(iii) A right angle triangle may have ...... line(s) of symmetry.

(iv) Alphabet Z has .... line of symmetry.

	(i)	(ii)	(iii)	(iv)
(a)	Sides	Circumference	1	Vertical
(b)	Diagonals	Boundary	2	No
(c)	Diagonals	Centre	1	No
(d)	Sides	Centre	3	Horizontal

24. How many figures has atleast two lines of symmetry?

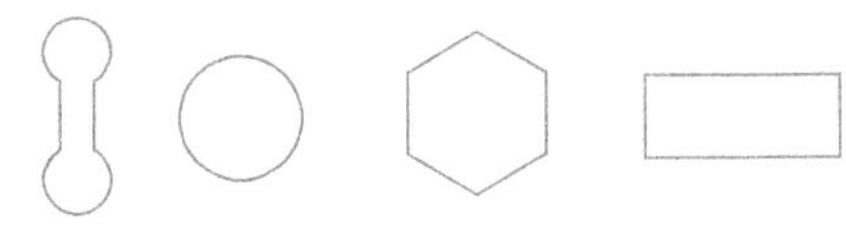

(a) 4   (b) 3

(c) 2   (d) 1

25. Which of the following is the reflection figure of the given figure?

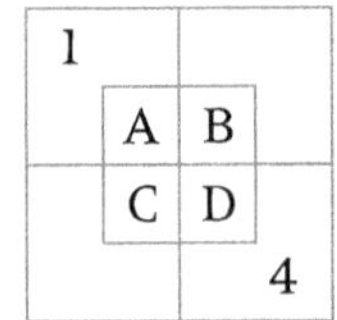

(a) 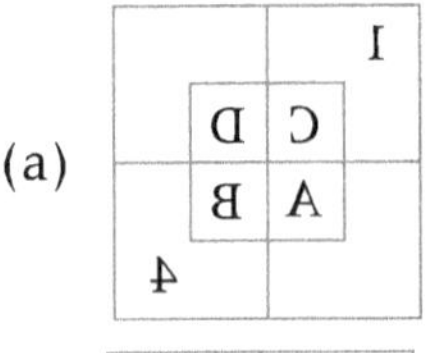   (b) 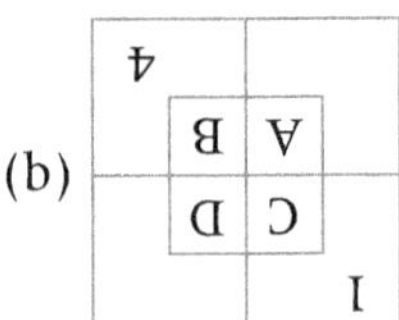

(c) 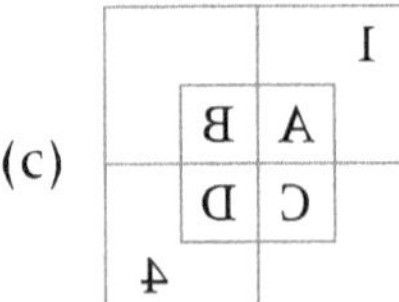   (d) 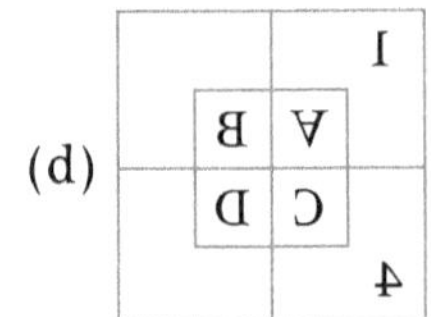

Mensuration

1 Mark Questions

Perimeter

1. A ΔABC is made by string. If the same string is used to make a square, then what will be the side of the square?

(a) 12 cm   (b) 7 cm

(c) 48 cm   (d) 36 cm

2. Which of the following figures has the greatest perimeter?

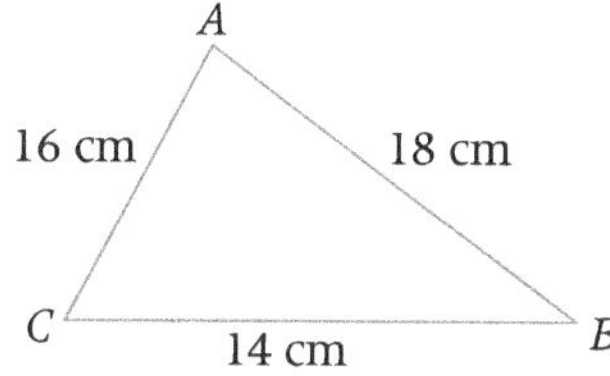

(a)

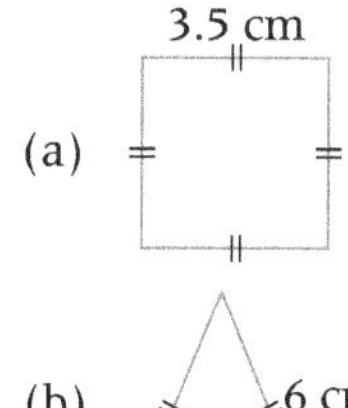

(b)

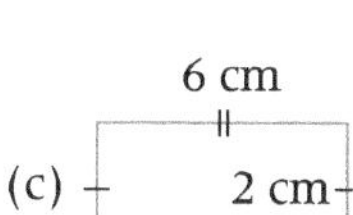

(c)

(d) Can't be determined

3. Rakesh Electronics Store is having a sale. To advertise the sale, the store manager wants to outline the store window of dimensions 9 m × 7 m with colourful ribbon. How many metres of ribbon will be needed to outline the 4 sides of the window?

(a) 35 m

(b) 24 m

(c) 19 m

(d) 32 m

4. Nitin wants to implant some vertical stones along the boundary of his plot at a distance of 12 m each. If length of the plot is 50 m and the breadth is 40 m, then the number of stones used is ....

(a) 450   (b) 45

(c) 15   (d) 12

5. The length and breadth of a rectangle is 32 m and 16 m respectively. If the perimeter of this rectangle is same as the perimeter of an equilateral triangle, then find the side of the equilateral triangle.

(a) 16 m

(b) 18 m

(c) 28 m

(d) 32 m

6. Find the perimeter of the following figures (not drawn to scale) and select the correct option.

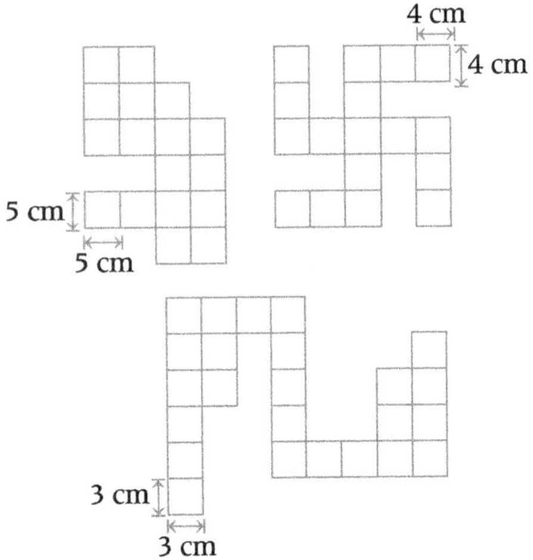

(a) Perimeter of [(i) + (ii)]
$\qquad$ = Perimeter of [(ii) + (iii)]
(b) Perimeter of [(i) + (ii)] = Perimeter of (iii)
(c) Perimeter of [(i) + (iii)] > Perimeter of (ii)
(d) None of the above

Area

7. The area of a rectangular park in 2600 m^2 and its breadth is 50 m. Find the distance covered by Rohan in going 3 times round the park.
   (a) 612 m $\qquad$ (b) 424 m
   (c) 336 m $\qquad$ (d) 636 m

8. The area of a rectangular field is 2688 m^2 and its length is 56 m. Find the cost of fencing the entire field, if the cost of fencing is ₹ 35/m.
   (a) ₹ 7120 $\qquad$ (b) ₹ 8280
   (c) ₹ 7280 $\qquad$ (d) ₹ 8430

9. If the breadth of the rectangle is 3 m and the rectangle and a square has equal area. Find the perimeter of the rectangle, if the length of side of the square is 12 m.

(a) 60 m $\qquad$ (b) 84 m
(c) 102 m $\qquad$ (d) 100 m

10. The perimeter of a rectangular field is 84 m. If the length of the field is 4 m more than thrice the breadth, then what is the (approx). area of the field?
    (a) 420 m^2 $\qquad$ (b) 410 m^2
    (c) 309 m^2 $\qquad$ (d) 310 m^2

11. A contractor constructed a big hall, rectangular in shape, with length 32 m and breadth 18 m. He wanted to buy 1 m by 1 m tiles. But in the shop 3 m by 2 m tiles only were available. How many tiles he has to buy for tiling the floor?
    (a) 48 $\qquad$ (b) 96
    (c) 120 $\qquad$ (d) 126

12. A floor of a hall is 10.5 m long and 4.5 m wide. A square carpet of sides 3.5 m is laid on the floor. Find the area of the floor that is not carpeted.
    (a) 30.5 m^2
    (b) 36.75 m^2
    (c) 35 m^2
    (d) 35.5 m^2

13. A rectangular piece of paper is folded as shown here. Find the area of the paper before it is folded.

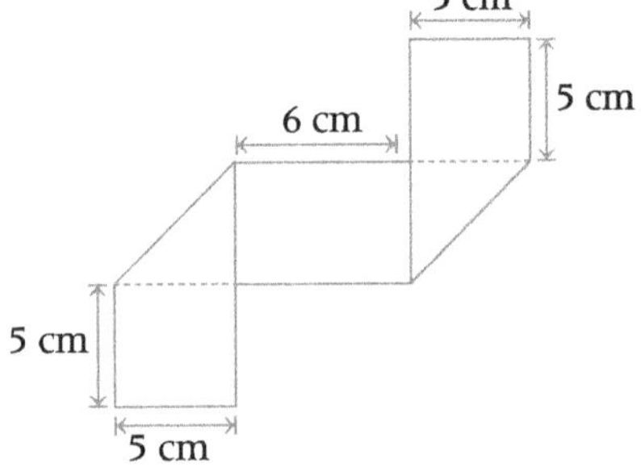

(a) 180 cm^2 $\qquad$ (b) 130 cm^2
(c) 22 cm^2 $\qquad$ (d) 84 cm^2

14. Find the area of the given figure (not drawn to scale).

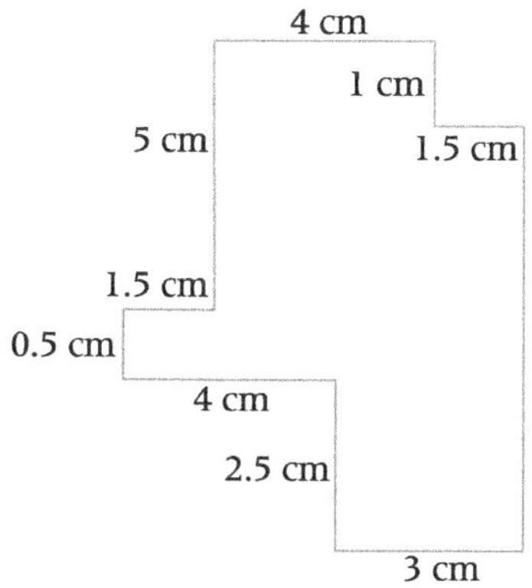

(a) 25.5 cm^2 (b) 37 cm^2
(c) 25 cm^2 (d) 39.75 cm^2

15. The figure *PRSU* is made up of three rectangles. The area of each rectangle is given inside the rectangles. If the length of *PQ* is 7 cm, then find the length of *US*.

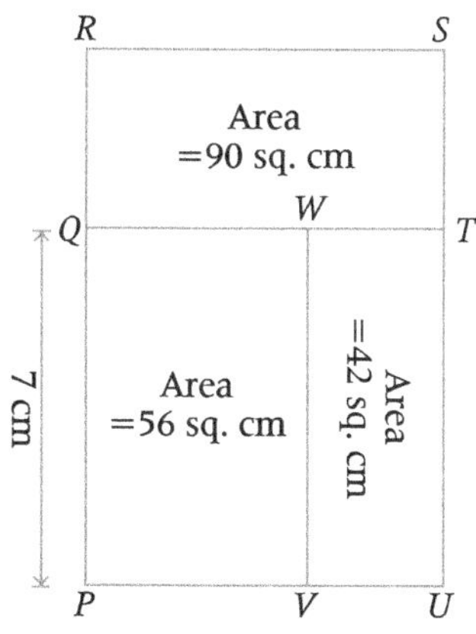

(a) 15 cm (b) 10 cm
(c) 12 cm (d) 5 cm

16. A road 4.5 m wide is built all around inside a square garden of side 169 m. What is the area of the remaining part of the garden?

(a) 22640 m^2 (b) 25600 m^2
(c) 24620 m^2 (d) 26480 m^2

17. *ABCD* is a rectangle. When the length and breadth of the rectangle are increased, the rectangle gets enlarged to *LNCM*. If the length of rectangle *ABCD* is thrice its breadth, then find the

(A) sum of perimeter of rectangle *ABCD* and *SNBA*.

(B) area of rectangle *LNCM*.

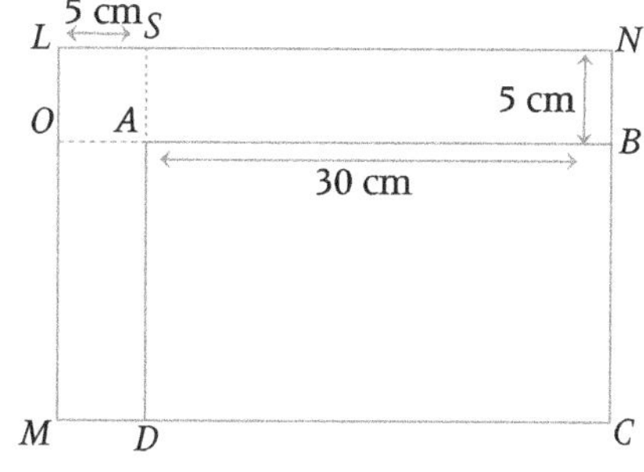

	(A)	(B)
(a)	180 cm	525 cm^2
(b)	220 cm	1000 cm^2
(c)	180 cm	625 cm^2
(d)	200 cm	650 cm^2

18. The given figure is made up of three squares. The side of the largest square is 12 cm. If the side of every consecutive square is half of its adjacent square, then find

(i) the perimeter of the figure.
(ii) the area of the figure.

	(i)	(ii)
(a)	69 cm	180 cm^2
(b)	63 cm	176 cm^2
(c)	66 cm	189 cm^2
(d)	63 cm	156 cm^2

2 Marks Questions

19. In the given figure (not drawn to scale), if *LMNQ* and *TUVW* are two identical squares, then find the area of the shaded region.

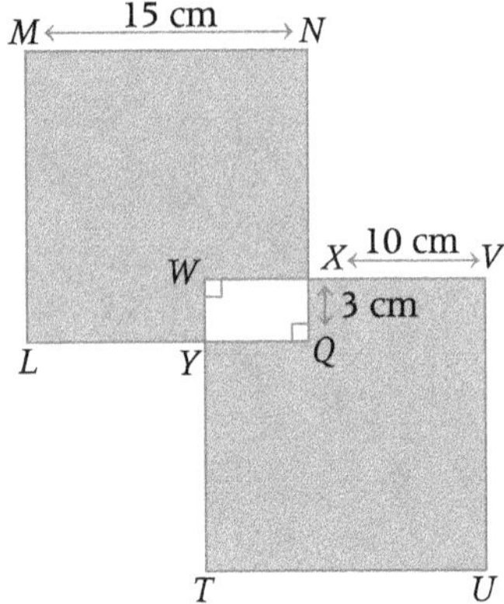

(a) 350 cm²

(b) 225 cm²

(c) 450 cm²

(d) 420 cm²

20. Find the area of the shaded region in the given figure (not drawn to scale).

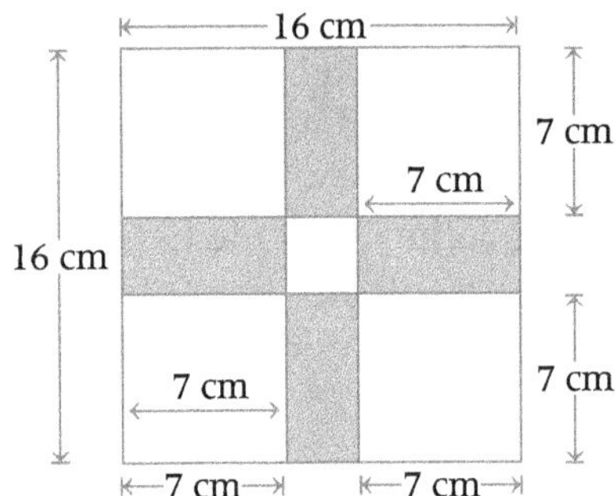

(a) 207 m²

(b) 58 m²

(c) 256 m²

(d) 56 m²

21. Which of the following figures has maximum shaded area?

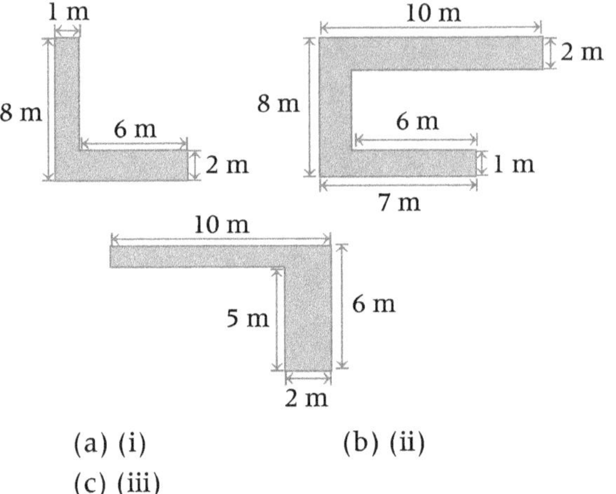

(a) (i)

(b) (ii)

(c) (iii)

(d) Can't be determined

22. Anu walks thrice around a square field of side 21 m. Manu walks thrice around a rectangular field of length 10 m and breadth 11 m. Who covers more distance and by how much?

(a) Manu, 20 m

(b) Anu, 126 m

(c) Manu, 176 m

(d) Anu, 176 m

23. Find the values of *P*, *Q* and *R*

S.No.	Length of rectangle (in m)	Breadth of rectangle (in m)	Area (in m²)	Perimeter (in m)
1.	19	*P*	247	64
2.	32	*Q*	*R*	98

	P	*Q*	*R*
(a)	12	17	544
(b)	13	12	272
(c)	15	15	272
(d)	13	17	544

Data Handling

1 Mark Questions

Tally Marks and Table Based Questions

1. The given table shows the number of vehicles owned by the families of a society.

No. of vehicles	Tally Marks
1	
2	
3	
4	
5	

How many more families have 2 vehicles than that have 5 vehicles?

(a) 6   (b) 8

(c) 5   (d) 4

Directions (Q. Nos. 2 and 3) *The favourite colour of sarees preferred by 33 women are shown below.*

Red, Brown, Green, Blue, Red, Grey, Black, Brown, Green, Red, Blue, Grey, Black, Blue, Brown, Green, Brown, Red, Blue, Red, Grey, Black, Black, Grey, Red, Red, Grey, Green, Red, Grey, Black, Blue, Red.

2. Find the total number of women who like Black and blue colour sarees.

(a) 6   (b) 8

(c) 10   (d) 14

3. How many more women like red colour saree than grey colour saree?

(a) 4   (b) 2

(c) 2   (d) 3

Pictograph Based Questions

Directions (Q. Nos. 4-6) Following is the pictograph of different kinds of trees in a garden.

Types of trees	Number of trees
Mango trees	
Coconut trees	
Banana trees	

Each   represents 15 trees.

4. Find the total number of trees in the garden.

(a) 190   (b) 180

(c) 230   (d) 225

5. The number of mango trees is .... times the number of banana trees.

(a) Ten   (b) Two

(c) Four   (d) Three

6. What is the difference between the number of mango trees and the number of banana trees?

(a) 40   (b) 30

(c) 80   (d) 60

Directions (Q. Nos. 7 and 8) The given pictograph shows mode of transport used by the number of people travel to various destinations. Study the pictograph carefully and answer the following questions.

Transport	Number of people
Bike	🧍🧍🧍🧍🧍🧍🧍🧍🧍🧍🧍🧍🧍
Bus	🧍🧍🧍🧍🧍🧍
Car	🧍🧍🧍🧍🧍🧍
Walk	🧍🧍🧍
Bicycle	🧍🧍🧍🧍🧍🧍
Key : 🧍 = 6 people , 🧍 = 3 people	

7. How many people did not travel by bus and car?

(a) 141   (b) 96

(c) 172   (d) 104

8. Which mode of transport was popular?

(a) Car

(b) Bike

(c) Bus

(d) Bicycle

Bar graph Based Questions

Directions (Q. Nos. 9 and 10) Study the given bar graph which shows the number of families having different kinds of pets and answer the following questions.

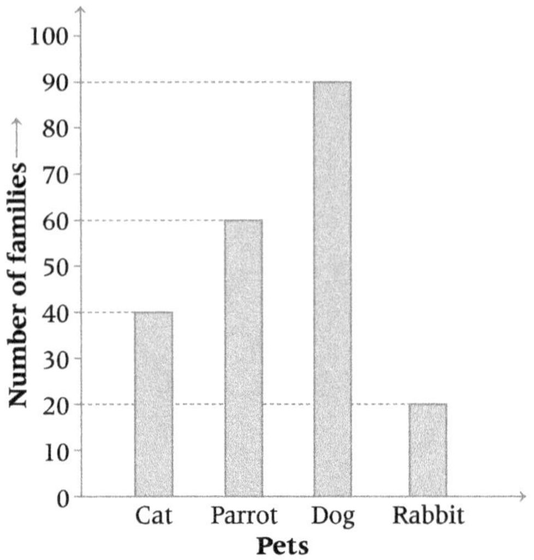

9. Which pet is with more than 60 families?

(a) Only Parrot

(b) Only Dog

(c) Only Car

(d) Both Parrot and Dog

10. What is the difference between the number of families who have a Cat and those who have a Parrot?

(a) 40   (b) 20   (c) 80   (d) 50

Directions (Q. Nos. 11 and 12) The given bar graph shows the height (in m) of 5 buildings. Study the graph carefully and answer the following questions.

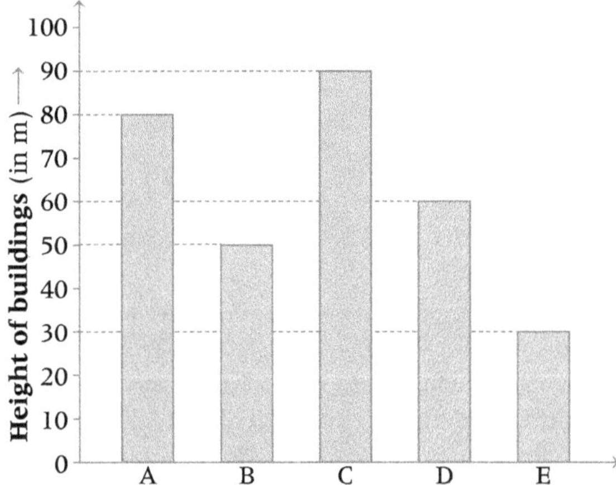

11. What is the total height of the tallest building and the shortest building?
(a) 120 m
(b) 140 m
(c) 150 m
(d) 160 m

12. How many buildings are of height greater than or equal to 50 m but less than 90 m?
(a) 4
(b) 3
(c) 2
(d) 1

Directions (Q. Nos. 13 and 14) The given bar graph shows the number of marks scored by Suraj in different subjects. Study the graph carefully and answer the following questions.

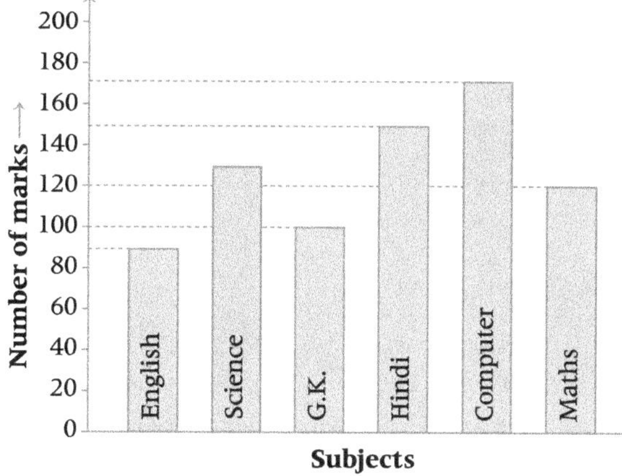

13. What fraction of the total marks scored by Suraj in Maths and Hindi together?
(a) $\dfrac{9}{25}$
(b) $\dfrac{4}{19}$
(c) $\dfrac{27}{76}$
(d) $\dfrac{23}{76}$

14. Find the difference between the total marks scored in Science and G.K. and English and Computer.
(a) 30
(b) 110
(c) 70
(d) 60

Directions (Q. Nos. 15 and 16) The given bar graph shows the number of t-shirts sold by a shopkeeper in six consecutive months. Study it carefully and answer the following questions.

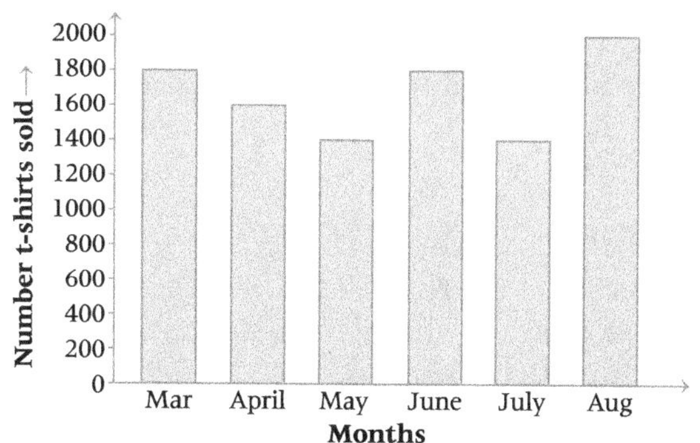

15. If the cost of 1 t-shirt is ₹ 400, then find the amount of money earned by shopkeeper in April and July altogether.
(a) ₹ 2100000
(b) ₹ 1200000
(c) ₹ 1920000
(d) ₹ 2500000

16. How many less number of t-shirts sold in May and July together than in March, June and August together?
(a) 2600
(b) 7500
(c) 5600
(d) 2800

Directions (Q. Nos. 17 and 18) The given bar graph shows the number of employees absent, in 4 departments in an office in one day. Study the given graph carefully and answer the given questions.

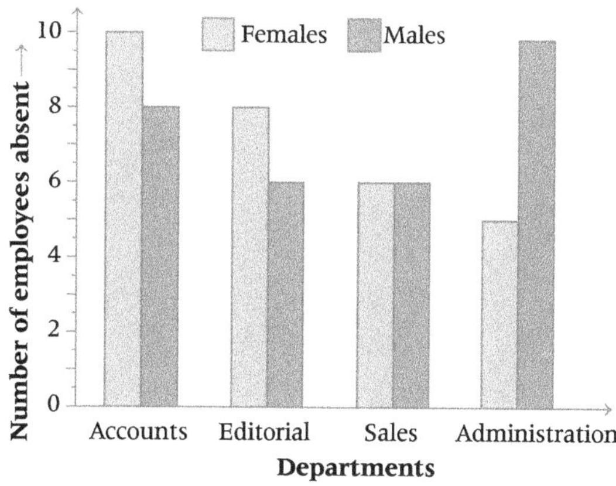

17. Which department has the maximum number of absent employees?
(a) Administration
(b) Accounts
(c) Editorial
(d) Sales

18. What is the ratio of total number of females to the total number of males absent in 4 departments?

(a) 2 : 5   (b) 3 : 4   (c) 1 : 1   (d) 1 : 3

Line graph Based Questions

Directions (Q. Nos. 19 and 20) The given line graph shows the number of students passed out from five schools A, B, C, D and E.

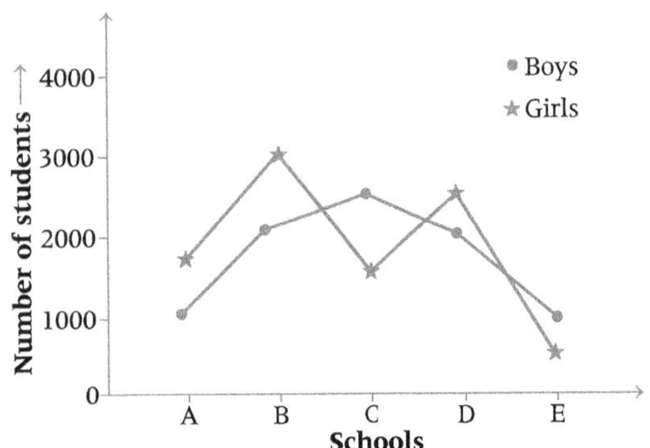

19. What fraction of the number of boys passed out from School B to the total number of boys passed out from all the schools together?

(a) $\dfrac{5}{16}$

(b) $\dfrac{7}{25}$

(c) $\dfrac{25}{8}$

(d) $\dfrac{4}{17}$

20. What is the difference between the total number of students passed out from School C and the total number of students passed out from School E?

(a) 1500   (b) 2500

(c) 1200   (d) 1000

2 Marks Questions

21. The given pictograph shows the sales of burgers in a week. Study the pictograph carefully and answer the following questions.

Days	Number of burgers sold
Monday	🍔 🍔 🍔 🍔
Tuesday	🍔 🍔 🍔 🍔 🍔
Wednesday	🍔 🍔
Thursday	🍔 🍔 🍔 🍔
Friday	🍔 🍔 🍔 🍔 🍔 🍔
Saturday	🍔 🍔 🍔 🍔 🍔 🍔 🍔

Each 🍔 represents 10 burgers

(i) On which day, were the most burgers sold?

(ii) How many less burgers sold on the last two days than the first four days?

(iii) If the cost of 1 burger is ₹ 30, then the money earned on Tuesday was ....

	(i)	(ii)	(iii)
(a)	Friday	10	₹ 3800
(b)	Saturday	20	₹ 1500
(c)	Monday	10	₹ 4200
(d)	Tuesday	10	₹ 4500

Directions (Q. Nos. 22-25) The given table shows the total number of students who applied for a competitive exam in five years.

Year	2016	2017	2018	2019	2021
Number of students	35000	35000	40000	65000	50000

If each ♀ represent 500 students, then answer the following questions.

22. How many symbols are needed to represent the number of students applied for the competitive exam in 2019?

(a) 130

(b) 145

(c) 115

(d) 120

23. There are .... symbols required to represent the total number of students applied from 2017 to 2021?

(a) 300

(b) 380

(c) 240

(d) 340

24. How many less symbols are needed to represent the number of students in 2016 than in 2019?

(a) 50 (b) 40

(c) 60 (d) 100

25. The given bar graph shows the weight of a container when empty and when different balls are placed in it. Find the total weight of balls P and Q.

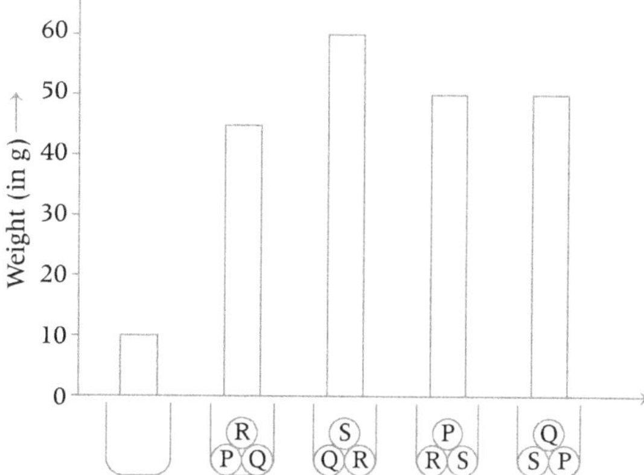

(a) 20 gm

(b) 15 gm

(c) 25 gm

(d) 35 gm

PRACTICE SET 01 

1. The product of the predecessor and successor of an even natural number is
   (a) divisible by 2 (b) divisible by 3
   (c) divisible by 4 (d) an odd number

2. The side of a square field is 65 m. What is the length of the fence required all around it?
   (a) 240 m (b) 260 m
   (c) 250 m (d) 280 m

Directions (Q. Nos. 3-5) Read the bar graph show in given figure and answer the following questions :

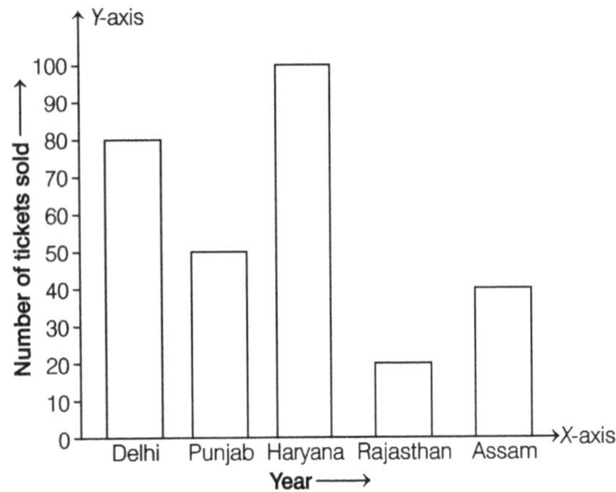

3. How many tickets of Assam State Lottery were sold by the agent?
   (a) 35 (b) 29
   (c) 40 (d) 45

4. What is the average number of tickets sold of all the states?
   (a) 58 (b) 56
   (c) 62 (d) 64

5. Consider the statement :
   The maximum number of tickets sold is 3 times the minimum number of tickets sold.
   (a) True (b) False
   (c) Don't know (d) None of these

6. Number of lines of symmetry in equilateral triangle is ?
   (a) 2 (b) 1
   (c) 6 (d) 3

7. The successor of 1 million is
   (a) 10001
   (b) 100001
   (c) 1000001
   (d) 10000001

8. How many circles can be drawn to pass through two given points?
   (a) 1
   (b) 2
   (c) 0
   (d) As many as possible

9. Kavita has 44 cassettes. She gives $\frac{3}{4}$ of them to Sonia. How many cassettes does Kavita keep?
   (a) 22 (b) 11
   (c) 14 (d) 13

10. Radhika's mother gave her ₹ 10.50 and her father gave her ₹ 15.80. Find the total amount given to Radhika by her parents.
    (a) ₹ 26.30 (b) ₹ 22.45
    (c) ₹ 24.50 (d) ₹ 28.30

11. The number of boys and girls in a school are 1168 and 1095 respectively. Express the ratio of the number of boys to that of the girls in the simplest form.
(a) 15 : 16   (b) 13 : 14
(c) 16 : 15   (d) 14 : 13

12. An isosceles trapezium has
(a) all sides equal
(b) parallel sides equal
(c) non-parallel sides equal
(d) any two sides equal

13. A bicycle wheel makes $4\frac{1}{2}$ turns. Find the number of right angles through which it turns.
(a) 14   (b) 16
(c) 18   (d) 24

14. Shikha painted 1/5 of the wall space in her room. Her brother Ravish helped and painted 3/5 of the wall space. How much the room is left unpainted?
(a) $\frac{2}{5}$ (b) $\frac{4}{5}$
(c) $\frac{1}{5}$ (d) $\frac{3}{5}$

15. The product of two numbers is 1530 and their HCF is 15. The LCM of these numbers is
(a) 102   (b) 120
(c) 84   (d) 112

16. Two sides of a triangle are 15 cm and 20 cm. The perimeter of the triangle is 50 cm. What is the 3rd side?
(a) 12 cm   (b) 18 cm
(c) 15 cm   (d) 24 cm

17. Number of lines of symmetry in Isosceles trapezium?
(a) 2   (b) 1
(c) 6   (d) 3

18. The product of the successor and predecessor of 99 is
(a) 9800   (b) 9900
(c) 1099   (d) 9700

19. Which digits have the same face value and place value in 92078634?
(a) 7 and 3   (b) 6 and 2
(c) 4 and 0   (a) 9 and 7

Directions (Q. Nos. 20-22) The sale of electric bulbs on different days of a week is shown below :

Days	Number of bulbs
Monday	🔆🔆🔆🔆🔆🔆
Tuesday	🔆🔆🔆🔆🔆🔆🔆🔆
Wednesday	🔆🔆🔆🔆
Thursday	🔆🔆🔆🔆🔆
Friday	🔆🔆🔆🔆🔆🔆🔆
Saturday	🔆🔆🔆🔆
Sunday	🔆🔆🔆🔆🔆🔆🔆🔆🔆

🔆 = 2 Bulbs

20. How many bulbs were sold on Friday?
(a) 14   (b) 16
(c) 20   (d) 18

21. If one bulb was sold at the rate of ₹ 10, what was the total earning on Sunday?
(a) ₹ 150   (b) ₹ 240
(c) ₹ 180   (d) ₹ 220

22. Find out the total earning of the week?
(a) ₹ 680   (b) ₹ 860
(c) ₹ 750   (d) ₹ 780

23. If a bicycle wheel has 48 spokes, then find the angle between a pair of adjacent spokes.
(a) 7.5   (b) 9
(c) 12   (d) 6.5

24. Rahul bought 4 kg 90 gm apples, 2 kg 60 gm of grapes and 5 kg 300 gm of mangoes. Find the weight of the fruits he bought in all.
(a) 13.520 kg   (b) 11.450 kg
(c) 12.360 kg   (d) 14.860 kg

25. The length of a steel tape for measurements of buildings is 10 m and its width is 2.4 cm. What is the ratio of its length to width?
(a) 3 : 1250   (b) 7 : 850
(c) 1250 : 3   (d) 850 : 7

26. A quadrilateral having two pairs of equal adjacent sides but unequal opposite sides is called a
(a) trapezium
(b) parallelogram
(c) kite
(d) rectangle

27. How many circles can be drawn to pass through three non-collinear points?
(a) 1
(b) 2
(c) 0
(d) As many as possible

28. Ramesh bought $2\dfrac{1}{2}$ kg sugar whereas Rohit bought $3\dfrac{1}{2}$ kg of sugar. Find the total quantity of sugar bought by both of them.
(a) 6 kg   (b) $\dfrac{11}{2}$ kg
(c) $\dfrac{15}{2}$ kg   (d) 7 kg

29. The least number divisible by each of the numbers 15, 20, 24 and 32 is
(a) 960   (b) 480   (c) 360   (d) 640

30. A square piece of land has each side equal to 100 m. If three layers of metal wire has to be used to fence it, what is the length of the wire needed?
(a) 1150 m   (b) 1250 m
(c) 1400 m   (d) 1200 m

31. Number of lines of symmetry in regular circle?
(a) 2   (b) 1
(c) 6   (d) infinite

32. If x and y are co-primes, then their LCM is
(a) 1   (b) $\dfrac{x}{y}$
(c) xy (d) None of these

33. Determine the difference of the place values of two 7's in 257839705.
(a) 6999999   (b) 6999000
(c) 6990500   (d) 6999300

34. A reflex angle measures
(a) more than 90° but less than 180°
(b) more than 180° but less than 270°
(c) more than 180° but less than 360°
(d) None of the above

35. Nasreen bought 3 m 20 cm cloth for shirt and 2 m 5 cm cloth for skirt. Find the total cloth bought by her.
(a) 5 m 35 cm   (b) 4 m 25 cm
(c) 5 m 25 cm   (d) 6 m 35 cm

36. An office opens at 9 am and closes at 5 pm with a lunch interval of 30 min. What is the ratio of lunch interval to the total period in office?
(a) 1 : 16   (b) 4 : 13
(c) 16 : 1   (d) 13 : 4

37. The teacher taught $\frac{3}{5}$ of the book, Vivek revised $\frac{1}{5}$ more on his own. How much does he still have to revise?
    (a) $\frac{5}{2}$ (b) $\frac{3}{5}$
    (c) $\frac{2}{5}$ (d) $\frac{5}{3}$

38. Which of the following numbers is a prime number?
    (a) 91
    (b) 81
    (c) 87
    (d) 97

39. Shikha runs around a square of side 75 m. Priya runs around a rectangle with length 60 m and breadth 45 m. Who covers the smaller distance and by how much?
    (a) Shikha, 150 m
    (b) Priya, 90 m
    (c) Shikha, 250 m
    (d) Priya, 210 m

40. The number of lines of symmetry of a kite is
    (a) 0 (b) 1
    (e) 2 (d) 3

41. Arvind fix fence wires in a garden, 70 m long and 50 m wide. Arvind bought metal pipes for posts. He fixed a post every 5 m apart. Each post was 2 m long. What is the total length of the pipes he bought for the posts?
    (a) 96 m (b) 84 m
    (c) 102 m (d) 112 m

42. a and b are two co-primes. Which of the following is/are true?
    (a) LCM $(a, b) = a \times b$
    (b) HCF $(a, b) = 1$
    (c) Both (a) and (b)
    (d) Neither (a) nor (b)

43. Ruchika bought some pens and exercise books for ₹ 107.00. There were 5 less pens than exercise books and each pen cost ₹ 25.00 and each exercise book cost ₹ 4.00, then the number of exercise books did she buy is equal to
    (a) 9 (b) 8
    (c) 10 (d) 12

44. Aakanksha, Banu and Katrina draw 3 cards each from 9 cards numbered from 1 to 9.
    [Aakanksha : A, Banu : B, Katrina = K]
    A : The product of my numbers is 48.
    B : The sum of my numbers is 15.
    K : The product of my numbers is 63.
    What is the largest number in the cards of Katrina?
    (a) 8 (b) 7
    (c) 9 (d) 6

45. Kareena had some nailpaints. She gave $\frac{1}{3}$ of them and 10 more nailpaints to Mala. She then gave $\frac{3}{4}$ of the remainder to Ankita but took back one nailpaint. If Kareena is left with 30 nailpaints, then how many nailpaints did she have at first?
    (a) 170 (b) 142
    (c) 159 (d) 189

46. What is the value of $\angle a + \angle b$ in the given figure?

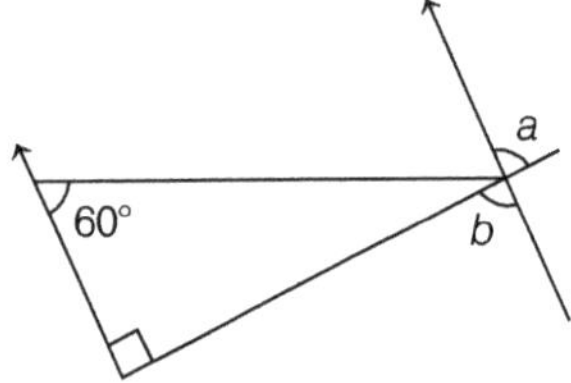

(a) 75°
(b) 90°
(c) 150°
(d) 180°

47. For the following statements, identify True (T) or False (F).

1. -4 is to the left of -10 on a number line.
2. $-100 > -50$
3. -1 lies on the left of 1
4. -11 is greater than -25

Codes

	1	2	3	4
(a)	F	F	T	T
(b)	F	T	F	T
(c)	T	F	T	T
(d)	T	T	F	T

48. Following figures are formed by joining six unit squares. Which figure has the smallest perimeter in given figures?

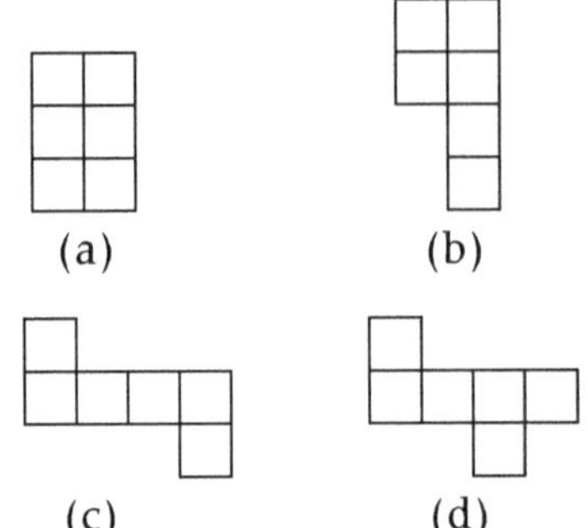

(a)   (b)

(c)   (d)

49. Which of the following is not equal to the others?

(a) $\dfrac{6}{8}$

(b) $\dfrac{12}{16}$

(c) $\dfrac{15}{25}$

(d) $\dfrac{18}{24}$

50. The choices of the fruits of 42 students in a class are as follows :

A, O, B, M, A, G, B, G, A, G, B, M, A, G, M, A, B, G, M, B, A, O, M, O, G, B, O, M, G, A, A, B, M, O, M, G, B, A, M, O, M, O,

where A, B, G, M and O stand for the fruits Apple, Banana, Grapes, Mango and Orange respectively. Which two fruits are liked by an equal number of students?

(a) A and M
(b) M and B
(c) B and O
(d) B and G

PRACTICE SET 

1. Harsimran bought $8m + 5n$ books from bookstore. If each m book costs ₹ 25.75 and each n book costs ₹ 35.75, then find the total cost of the books.
   (a) ₹ 384.75
   (b) ₹ 392.25
   (c) ₹ 350.25
   (d) None of the above

2. Simplify and choose the correct option.
   $$9 + [9z - \{6 + 3y - (2z - 3y) - 3\}]$$
   (a) $21z + 18y + 12$
   (b) $18y - 21z - 12$
   (c) $11z + 9y - 6$
   (d) $11z - 6y + 6$

3. A vessel has 5 liters and 500 mL of juice. How many glasses each of capacity 25 mL can be filled with the given quantity of milk?
   (a) 240
   (b) 230
   (c) 220
   (d) 180

4. Mrs. Banerjee prepared a dessert in the given ratio as per the table. Fill in the missing numbers in the table.

Number of spoons of sugar	4	10	15	-	24
Number of spoons of gelaten	12	30	-	54	-

   (a) 45, 18, 72
   (b) 60, 20, 68
   (c) 30, 60, 90
   (d) 45, 20, 60

5. Evaluate the following expression and choose the correct option, if $a = 2, b = 4$ and $c = -1$.
   $$(ab - ac) \div abc$$
   (a) $-\dfrac{2}{3}$
   (b) $-\dfrac{5}{4}$
   (c) $\dfrac{7}{6}$
   (d) None of these

6. What is the missing value in the box?
   $$1\frac{2}{4} + \square = 2\frac{3}{12}$$
   (a) $\dfrac{5}{12}$
   (b) $\dfrac{5}{4}$
   (c) $\dfrac{7}{12}$
   (d) $\dfrac{9}{12}$

7. **Statement** Two numbers have 16 as HCF and 308 as LCM. The statement is
   (a) true
   (b) false
   (c) No conclusion can be drawn.
   (d) None of the above

8. The line which divides a circle equally is called
   (a) Chord
   (b) Radius
   (c) Secant
   (d) Diameter

9. The number of star fish and gold fish in an aquarium is in the ratio 3 : 7. After adding 25 more gold fish into the aquarium, the new ratio of the star fish to gold fish became 6 : 19. How many star fish and gold fish are there in the aquarium now?
   (a) 30, 70
   (b) 60, 140
   (c) 3, 7
   (d) None of these

10. Number name for 700900800 is
    (a) Seven nine and eight
    (b) Seven crore nine thousand and eight hundred
    (c) Seventy crore nine lakh and eight hundred
    (d) None of the above

11. What is the difference between $\dfrac{2}{3}$ of 16 and $\dfrac{1}{18} \div \dfrac{1}{3}$?

(a) $10\dfrac{1}{2}$

(b) $\dfrac{17}{2}$

(c) $\dfrac{19}{4}$

(d) None of these

12. Vessels P and Q have 145 litres and 116 litres of liquid, respectively. What should be the volume of the largest possible container which can measure out the liquid exact number of times?

(a) 1 litre

(b) 29 litres

(c) 4 litres

(d) None of these

13. If 27432* is divisible by 6, then least value of * is

(a) 0   (b) 6

(c) 2   (d) 4

14. Niharika finds the average of her three most recent badminton scores by using following expression, where a, b and c are the three scores: $\dfrac{a+b+c}{3} \times 100$.

Which of the following would also determine the average of her scores?

(a) $\left(\dfrac{a}{3} + \dfrac{b}{3} + \dfrac{c}{3}\right) \times 100$

(b) $\dfrac{(a+b+c) \times 3}{100}$

(c) $\dfrac{a+b+c}{3}$

(d) $\dfrac{a+b+c}{3} + 100$

15. Which of the following is divisible by 11?

(a) 234612

(b) 1101123

(c) 1122334

(d) None of the above

16. Given that $\angle AOB$ is a right angle, find the measure of $\angle AOC$ and $\angle COB$.

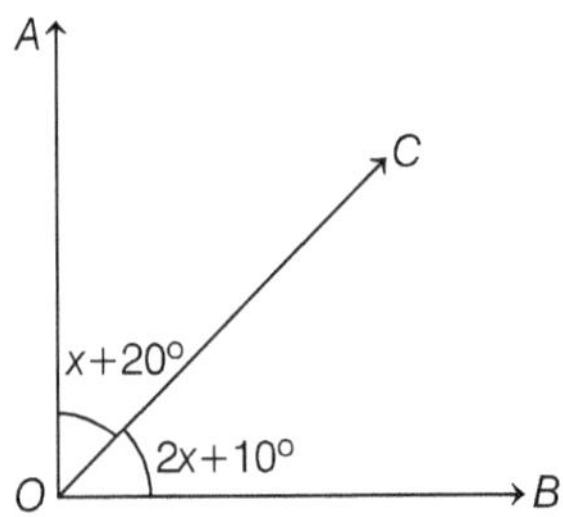

(a) 70° and 20°   (b) 30° and 60°

(c) 45° and 45°   (d) 40° and 50°

17. If $a \Delta b = 7 \times a - 3 \times b$, then $6 \Delta 4$ is equal to

(a) 25   (b) 30

(c) 40   (d) 50

18. The smallest number which when divide by 30, 35, 45 and 50 leaves remainders 24, 29, 39 and 44, respectively is

(a) 3150   (b) 3144

(c) 3462   (d) 3223

19. A tank was 0.2 full. When another 600 mL of water was poured into the tank, it became half full.

How much water was in the tank at first?

(a) 2 liters

(b) 250 mL

(c) 750 mL

(d) 3.5 liters

20. If $x = 2, y = 3$ and $z = -2$, then the value of $4x + 6z - (x + 3y - 3x) + 5y$ will be
(a) 4
(b) 5
(c) 6
(d) 8

21. What are the values of $\angle b$ and $\angle c$?

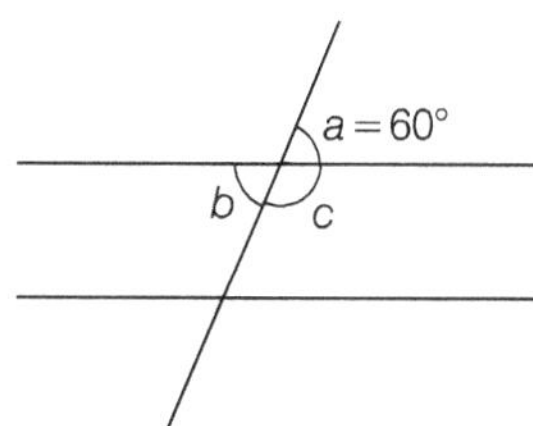

(a) 60° and 120°
(b) 60° and 60°
(c) 120° and 60°
(d) 120° and 120°

22. If a number is divisible by two coprime numbers, then it is divisible by their .... also.
(a) sum
(b) difference
(c) product
(d) multiple

23. A group of 30 persons can consume 48 kg of rice in 4 days. In how many days can 40 persons consume 240 kg of rice?
(a) 30
(b) 25
(c) 15
(d) None of these

24. An angle exceeds its supplement by 40°. The measure of the angle is
(a) 70°
(b) 80°
(c) 110°
(d) 100°

25. The difference of largest 4-digit number and smallest 4-digit number formed using 5, 0, 2,8 is
(a) 2058
(b) 6462
(c) 10578
(d) 8520

26. How much simple interest is earned on ₹ 300 deposited for 20 months in a saving account paying 15% simple interest annually?

$$\left(\text{Simple Interest} = \frac{\text{Principle} \times \text{Rate} \times \text{Time}}{100} \right)$$

(a) ₹ 50
(b) ₹ 75
(c) ₹ 90
(d) None of these

27. Choose the correct expanded form of 970429 in the following options.
(a) $9 \times 100000 + 7 \times 10000 + 4 \times 1000 + 2 \times 10 + 9 \times 1$
(b) $9 \times 10000 + 7 \times 1000 + 4 \times 100 + 2 \times 10 + 9 \times 1$
(c) $9 \times 100000 + 7 \times 10000 + 4 \times 100 + 2 \times 10 + 9 \times 1$
(d) None of the above

28. Simplify and choose the correct option.
$$52 - [2 - 3\{4 + (7 - 8) - \overline{2 + 7}\} - 4]$$
(a) 36
(b) 46
(c) 50
(d) 72

29. There are 4 lines in a plane, two of which are parallel. The maximum number of points in which they can intersect is
(a) 4
(b) 5
(c) 6
(d) 8

30. What must be added to the numbers 7, 16, 43 and 79, so that they become proportional?
(a) 4
(b) 5
(c) 10
(d) None of these

31. A company's quality control department four an average of 10 defective models for every 1500 models that were checked. If the company produces 75000 models in a year, then how many of them would be expected to be defective?
(a) 1000
(b) 500
(c) 250
(d) None of these

32. Find the least number which when divided by 8, 20 and 24 leaves remainder 7 in each case
(a) 127
(b) 120
(c) 113
(d) None of these

33. An angle which is greater than 180° but less than 360° is called
(a) Obtuse angle
(b) Complete angle
(c) Reflex angle
(d) None of the above

34. Which of the following is the lists of three consecutive even integers whose sum is 30?
(a) 9, 10 and 11   (b) 8, 10 and 12
(c) 8, 9 and 13   (d) 6, 10 and 14

35. The sum of given expression is
$(-182) + (-30) + 6 + (-721) - (+432) + 700 - (-17)$
(a) 462   (b) 392   (c) -246 (d) -642

36. The length, breadth and height of a room are 825 cm, 675 cm and 450 cm, respectively. What is the length of the tape that can measure the three dimensions of the room?
(a) 75 cm   (b) 150 cm
(c) 300 cm   (d) 600 cm

37. Number of diagonals in a octagon are
(a) 24   (b) 28
(c) 20   (d) None of these

38. If $4x$ means $1 \times 2 \times 3 \times 4$, then $4x = 24$ and, if $5x$ means $1 \times 2 \times 3 \times 4 \times 5$, then $5x = 120$, find the value of $6x$.
(a) 720   (b) 240   (c) 360   (d) 120

39. If $u \nabla v = \dfrac{10}{u} - \dfrac{12}{v}$, then $3 \nabla 7$ is equal to
(a) $\dfrac{10}{7}$ (b) $\dfrac{12}{3}$ (c) $\dfrac{34}{21}$ (d) $\dfrac{21}{8}$

40. Neel spent 0.3 of its money on Monday, 0.4 of it on Tuesday and ₹ 40 on Wednesday. He then found that he had ₹ 50 left. How much did he spend altogether on Monday and Tuesday?
(a) ₹ 240   (b) ₹ 750
(c) ₹ 210   (d) ₹ 900

41. There are two boxes of chocolates, X and Y. The ratio of weight of X to weight of Y is 4 : 1. If 39 of chocolates is transferred from X to Y, then the ratio-of weight of X to weight of Y is 7 : 5. Find the total weight of the two boxes of chocolates.
(a) 36   (b) 144
(c) 180   (d) 72

42. Find the smallest possible value of the number 368 ⊠◯⬦ So that it is divisible by 3, 4 and 25.

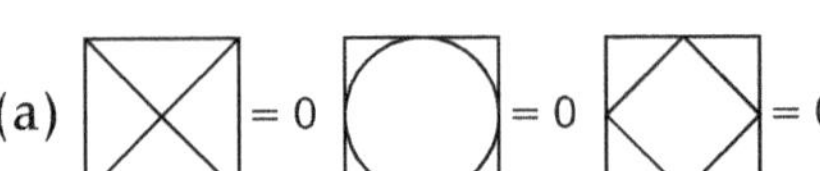
(a) ⊠ = 0   ◯ = 0   ⬦ = 0

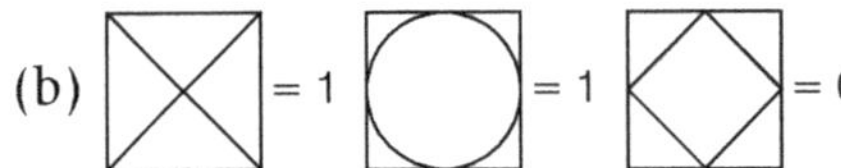
(b) ⊠ = 1   ◯ = 1   ⬦ = 0

(c) ⊠ = 0   ◯ = 0   ⬦ = 4

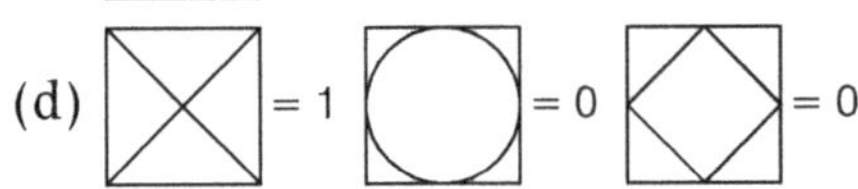
(d) ⊠ = 1   ◯ = 0   ⬦ = 0

43. In the given figure,
$\angle YXM = \angle MXN = \angle NXZ$

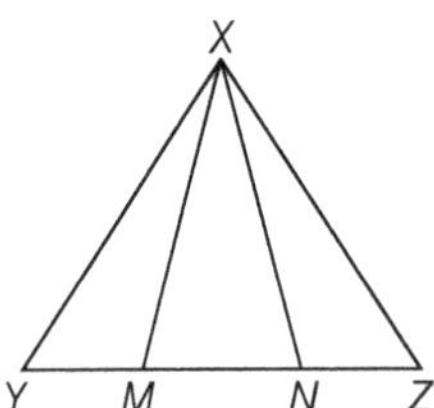

Then, which of the following statements is true?
(a) XM is bisector of $\angle YXN$.
(b) XN is bisector of $\angle MXZ$.
(c) XM and XN are trisector of $\angle YXZ$.
(d) All of the above

44. In the given figure, $EO \perp AB$ and $FO \perp CD$. Given that, $\angle AOD = 120°$, what is the value of $\angle EOF$?

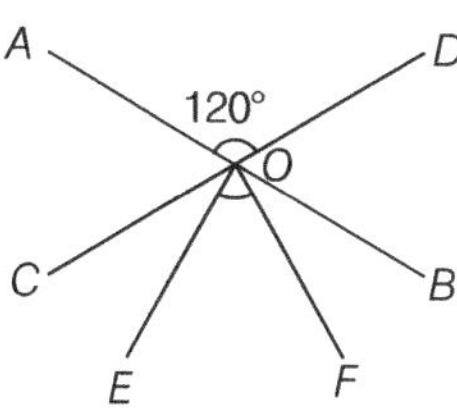

(a) 10°   (b) 30°   (c) 60°   (d) 90°

45. Simplify and choose the correct option of

$$\dfrac{\dfrac{2}{5} + \dfrac{1}{4}}{\dfrac{3}{8} \times \dfrac{4}{5} - 1\dfrac{9}{10}}$$

(a) $\dfrac{7}{10}$ (b) $\dfrac{14}{26}$

(c) $\dfrac{13}{20}$ (d) None of these

46. $-4 + 3[24 - (-2.5) \times 8 \div (-1.8 - 0.2)$

The value of the given expression is equal to

(a) 38   (b) 46
(c) 52   (d) None of these

47. The number of obtuse angle in given figure is

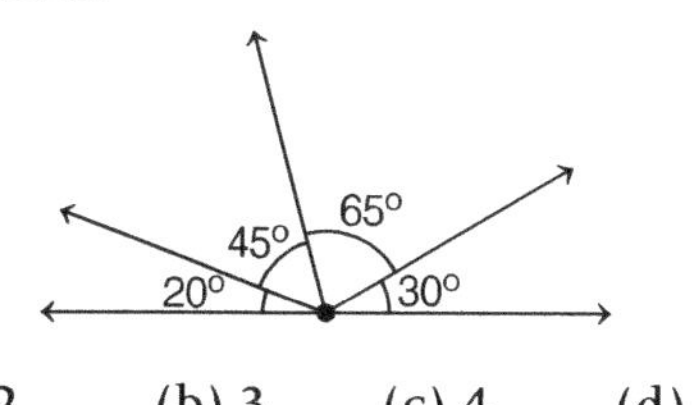

(a) 2   (b) 3   (c) 4   (d) 5

48. Length and breadth of a rectangular sheet of paper are 20 cm and 10 cm, respectively. A rectangular piece is cut from the sheet as shown in given figure. Which of the following statements is correct for the remaining sheet?

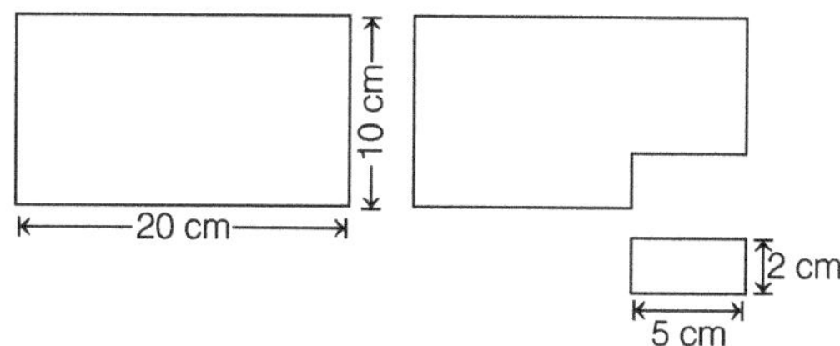

(a) Perimeter remains same but area changes.
(b) Area remains the same but perimeter changes.
(c) Both area and perimeter are changing.
(d) Both area and perimeter remain the same.

49. Savitri has a sum of ₹ x. She spent ₹ 1000 on grocery, ₹ 500 on clothes and ₹ 400 on education, and received ₹ 200 as a gift. How much money (in ₹) is left with her?

(a) $x - 1700$ (b) $x - 1900$
(c) $x + 200$ (d) $x - 2100$

50. Saturn and Jupiter take 9 h 56 min and 10 h 40 min, respectively for one spin on their axes. The ratio of the time taken by Saturn and Jupiter in lowest form is _.

(a) 160 : 149   (b) 131 : 150
(c) 149 : 160   (d) 150 : 131

HINTS & SOLUTIONS

Chapter 1 : Numbers

1. *(b)* In the international numeration system, a comma is used after every 3-digits or places from right.

$\therefore$ Required number = 1,832,480

2. *(c)* Here, 1798 and 9781 are the numbers with 7 at the hundreds place in given numbers.

In both numbers, 9781 is the greatest number with 7 at the hundreds place.

3. *(c)* Place value of 5 in 79502 = $5 \times 100 = 500$

Face value of 5 in 79502 = 5

$\therefore$ Required difference = $500 - 5 = 495$

4. *(c)* Greatest 4-digit number formed by 5, 0, 2 and 6 = 6520

[write the digits in descending order]

Smallest 4-digit number formed by 5, 0, 2 and 6 = 2056

[To write the digits in ascending order out of 0 and write 0 on 2nd place from left.]

5. *(c)* The greatest 5-digits number formed by the digits 2, 7, 8, 9 and 0 = 98720

[write the digits in descending order]

6. *(c)*

TTh	Th	H	T	O
6	9	0	4	6

$\therefore$ Expanded form of 69046

$$= 6 \times 10000 + 9 \times 1000 + 0 \times 100$$
$$+ 4 \times 10 + 6 \times 1$$
$$= 60000 + 9000 + 40 + 6$$

7. *(b)* Given number write the standard form of international system.

$$85, 423, 610$$

$\therefore$ 85 millions are there in 85423610.

8. *(c)* In the given pattern, the least/smallest number is chosen.

$\therefore$ In the sequence 89426, 82946, 82469, 86429 the smallest number is 82469.

9. (b) I. Commas are inserted in a number after each <u>Period</u>.

II. The first basic roman numeral is I.

III. <u>Face</u> value of a number is the number itself.

IV. 1000 = <u>10</u> hundred.

V. 1 lakh = <u>100</u> thousands.

10. *(a)* Rounding off 11793 to nearest hundreds

$$= 11800$$

Rounding off 9372 to nearest hundreds = 9400

$\therefore$ Difference $= 11800 - 9400 = 2400$

11. *(d)* Rounding off 3239 to nearest tens = 3240

Rounding off 38 to nearest tens = 40

$\therefore$ Product = $3240 \times 40 = 129600$

12. *(c)* I. 72946 rounded off to nearest thousand is 73000.

II. 46230 rounded off to nearest thousand is 46000.

III. 58996 rounded off to nearest thousand is 59000.

IV. 62341 rounded off to nearest thousand is 62000.

Hence, 58996 in incorrectly matched.

13. *(c)* Imports of the country in year 2014

$$= 746493$$

Rounding off to nearest thousands

$$= 746000$$

Exports of the country in year 2014

$$= 634629$$

Rounding off to nearest thousands

$$= 635000$$

$\therefore$ Difference = $746000 - 635000 = 111000$

14. *(b)* Difference = $600 - 200 = 400$

$$= 500 - 100 = CD$$

[$\because$ In Roman Numeral, D = 500 and C = 100]

15. *(a)* Smallest 3-digit number = 100

Greatest 2-digit number = 99

$\therefore$ Difference = $100 - 99 = 1 = I$ [in roman]

16. *(a)* Meenakshi's date of Joining her job

$$= 29 \text{ th December} = 20 + 9 = XXIX$$

17. *(b)* We have,   XIX $= 19$

XCIX $= 99$

LXXV $= 75$

$\because 99 > 75 > 19$.

$\therefore$ Descending order $=$ XCIX $>$ LXXV $>$ XIX

18. *(c)* Length of cloth $= 55$ m 20 cm

$= 5500$ cm $+ 20$ cm

$[\because 1$ m $= 100$ cm$]$

$= 5520$ cm

Number of shirts to be made $= 15$

$\therefore$ Length of cloth used in one shirt

$= \dfrac{\text{Length of cloth being used}}{\text{Number of shirts to be made}}$

$= \dfrac{5520}{15} = 368$ cm

$= 300$ cm $+ 68$ cm $= 3$ m 68 cm

19. *(b)* Considering option (b) Factors of $12 = 1, 2, 3, 4, 6, 12$

Sum of factors (except 12)

$= 1 + 2 + 3 + 4 + 6 = 16 > 12$

Hence, option (b) is correct.

20. *(b)* Prime factorisation of $20 = 2 \times 2 \times 5$

Multiples of $2 = 2, 4, 6, 8, 10$

$\therefore 5$ is a factor of 20 but not a multiple of 2.

21. *(c)* Common multiples of both 3 and 5 in the 1st 100 natural numbers

$=$ Multiples of $(3 \times 5) =$ Multiples of 15

$= 15, 30, 45, 60, 75, 90$

$\therefore$ Required number of multiples is 6.

22. *(a)* Given, a is the factor of b i.e., a divides b.

and c is the multiple of b, i.e., b divides c.

$\therefore a$ divides c.

e.g. 2 is a factor of 4 and 8 is the multiple of 4.

$\therefore 2$ divides 8.

23. *(c)* Given, $a + b = 39$

where a and b are prime numbers.

$\therefore \qquad a = 2$

and $\qquad b = 37$

So, $a \times b = 2 \times 37 = 74$

24. *(b)* Factors of $16 = 1, 2, 4, 8, 16$

Factors of $14 = 1, 2, 7, 14$

Factors of $18 = 1, 2, 3, 9, 6, 18$

$\therefore 14$ has exactly 4 factors.

25. *(a)* Required number

$=$ HCF of $(33 - 3, 63 - 3, 75 - 3)$

$=$ HCF of $(30, 60, 72)$

$30 = 2 \times 3 \times 5,$

$60 = 2 \times 2 \times 3 \times 5$

$72 = 2 \times 2 \times 2 \times 3 \times 3$

$\therefore$ Required number

$=$ HCF of $(30, 60, 72) = 2 \times 3 = 6$

26. *(a)* Number of cards of each type to be placed

$=$ HCF $(45, 30)$

$=$ HCF $(3 \times 3 \times 5, 2 \times 3 \times 5)$

$= 3 \times 5 = 15$

27. *(d)* 23 and 29 are both coprime numbers.

$\therefore$ LCM of 23 and $29 = 23 \times 29$

$[\because$ LCM of two coprime numbers is their product$]$

Hence, A is false and R is the correct but it is not explanation of A.

28. *(c)* I. The numbers which have more than two factors are called <u>Composite Numbers.</u>

[Match (iii)]

II. HCF of two coprime number is 1.

[Match (i)]

III. The numbers which have only two factors (1 and itself) are called <u>Prime Numbers.</u>

[Match (iv)]

IV. The LCM of a number is x and HCF is y, then product of numbers is xy (Product of <u>HCF $\times$ LCM</u>).   [Match (v)]

29. *(c)* I. Smallest prime number is even.

[Match (iii)]

II. $2n + 1$ is the general form of an odd number.

[Match (i)]

III. HCF of two or more prime numbers is one.

[Match (ii)]

IV. 0 has no multiples.   [Match (iv)]

30. *(d)* Number of participants in football = 60

Number of participants in basketball = 84

Number of participants in running = 108

Required number of participants in each room

$$= \text{HCF } (60, 84, 108)$$

Now, $60 = 2 \times 2 \times 3 \times 5$

$84 = 2 \times 2 \times 3 \times 7$

$108 = 2 \times 2 \times 3 \times 3 \times 3$

$\therefore \quad \text{HCF} = 2 \times 2 \times 3 = 12$

So, number of rooms required

$$= \frac{60 + 84 + 108}{12} = \frac{252}{12} = 21$$

31. *(b)* Given, HCF of two numbers = 46

LCM of two numbers = 368

and $\qquad 46 = \dfrac{\text{Ist number}}{2}$

$\therefore \qquad$ Ist number $= 46 \times 2 = 92$

Let the other number be x.

We know that, product of two numbers

$$= \text{Their HCF} \times \text{Their LCM}$$

$\Rightarrow \qquad 92 \times x = 46 \times 368$

$\therefore \qquad x = \dfrac{46 \times 368}{92} = 184$

32. *(c)* According to the question,

Place value of 5 = 5000

and place value of 3 = 6 times 5000

$$= 6 \times 5000 = 30000$$

$\therefore$ Required Number = 30000 + 5000 = 35000

33. *(d)* Using digits 3, 1, 2, 8 and 6 only once, the greatest 5-digit number = 86321

$\therefore$ Place value of 6 in 86321

$$= 6 \times 1000 = 6000$$

Using digit 3, 1, 2, 8 and 6 only once, the smallest 5-digit number = 12368

$\therefore$ Place value of 6 in 12368 $= 6 \times 10 = 60$

So, required difference = 6000 − 60 = 5940

34. *(d)* Weight of 50 pencil boxes

$= 1 \text{ kg } 250 \text{ gm}$

$= 1000 \text{ gm} + 250 \text{ gm} \qquad [\because 1 \text{kg} = 1000 \text{ gm}]$

$= 1250 \text{ gm}$

$\therefore$ Weight of 1 pencil box

$$= \frac{1250}{50} = 25 \text{ gm}$$

Capacity of wooden box = 800 gm

$\therefore$ Number of pencil boxes that can be packed

$$= \frac{800}{25} = 32$$

35. *(c)* **Statement I**, "If a number is divisible by another number, then it is divisible by each of the factors of that number" is true.

e.g. 108 is divisible by 12, then 108 is also divisible by each of the factors of 12 (they are 2, 3, 4 and 6).

Statement II The least number = LCM of $(12, 15, 20 \text{ and } 27) - K = 540 - 4 = 536$

Where $K = 12 - 8 = 15 - 11$

$$= 20 - 16 = 27 - 23 = 4$$

"The least number which when divided by 12, 15, 20 and 27 leaves remainder 8, 11, 16 and 23 respectively is 536" is true.

36. *(a)* LCM of 2, 3, 4, 5 and 6 = 60

Now, we want to find a number which is completely divisible by 7 but when it is divided by 2, 3, 4, 5 and 6 respectively, it leaves remainder 1.

$\therefore$ Required number = $60 K + 1$

$$[K \text{ is an integer}]$$

$$= 60 \times 5 + 1 \qquad [K = 5]$$

$$= 301$$

37. *(d)* Cost of 1 flat in Building *A*

$= ₹ 25680$

$\therefore$ Cost of 35 flats in Building *A*

$= ₹ 25680 \times 35$

$= ₹ 898800$

Cost of 1 flat in Building B = ₹ 302800

$\therefore$ Cost of 55 flats in Building *B*

$= 302800 \times 55$

$= ₹ 16654000$

$\therefore$ Difference between all flats of *A* and *B*

$= 16654000 - 898800$

$= ₹ 15755200$

Chapter 2 : Whole Numbers

1. *(c)* I. All whole numbers are not natural numbers.

So, statement I is not true.

II. Statement II is true.

III. Statement III is true.

2. *(d)* The smallest whole number is 0, then point A represents 0.

∴ The point B represents of 11.

3. *(c)* Since, first jump is 0-6 and second jump is 6-12.

Therefore, this is a multiplication of 6 and 2.

∴ $\qquad 6 \times 2 = 12$

4. *(a)* $\dfrac{a}{b} = 0$ is only possible, when $a = 0$ because

if $b = 0$, $\dfrac{a}{b}$ can not be defined.

5. *(b)* We know, 1 million $= 1000000$

∴ Predecessor of 1 million $= 1000000 - 1$
$$= 999999$$

6. (c) Given, whole number $= 7510001$

The three consecutive whole numbers that come just before it will be predecessors of this number.

Predecessor of 7510001
$$= 7510001 - 1 = 7510000$$
Predecessor of 7510000
$$= 7510000 - 1 = 7509999$$
Predecessor of 7509999
$$= 7509999 - 1 = 7509998$$
Hence, option (c) is correct.

7. *(b)* Given, number $= 199$

Predecessor $= 199 - 1 = 198$

Successor $= 199 + 1 = 200$

Product $= 198 \times 200 = 39600$

8. *(c)* We know, 1 lakh $= 100000$

Predecessor of 1 lakh $= 100000 - 1 = 99999$

Successor of 99999 $= 99999 + 1 = 100000$

∴ Successor of predecessor of 1 lakh is itself.

9. *(d)* All of the given properties are satisfied by whole numbers under multiplication.

10. *(a)* If p and q are two whole numbers then from commutative property under subtraction $p - q = q - p = 0$, if $p = q$.

11. *(c)* Since, we know commutative property under addition is stated as, $x + y = y + x$, where x and y are any two whole numbers.

∴ $14 + 16 = 16 + 14$ is true.

12. *(d)* $72(7 + 3) = 72 \times 7 + 72 \times 3$ is an example of distributive property of multiplication over addition.

13. *(a)* $129 \times 30 + 129 \times 10 = 129(30 + 10)$, it is the form of distributive property.

14. *(c)*

I. $5 + 6$ is a whole number $\rightarrow$ Closed under addition property.

II. $12 \times (15 \times 9) = (12 \times 15) \times 19 \rightarrow$ Associative property.

III. $14 \times (20 - 1) = 14 \times 20 - 14 \times 1 \rightarrow$ Distributive property.

IV. $14 \times 16 = 16 \times 14 \rightarrow$ Commutative property.

V. $1 \rightarrow$ Multiplicative identity.

VI. $0 \rightarrow$ Additive identity.

15. *(a)* Given, fixed cost $= ₹\ 17$

Cost per cm $= ₹\ 5$

Length of the frame $= 15$ cm

∴ Total cost $= 17 + (5 \times 15)$

16. *(a)* Number of packets sold on Monday $= 40$

Number of packets sold on Tuesday $= 60$

Cost of each packet $= ₹\ 25$

∴ Total amount $= 25 \times 40 + 25 \times 60$
$$= 25 \times (40 + 60)$$

17. *(b)* Given, $5476a$ is divisible by 3, then
$5 + 4 + 7 + 6 + a$ is divisible by 3.

∴ $22 + a$ is divisible by 3.

Now, $a = 2$ so that, $22 + a = 22 + 2 = 24$

which is divisible by 3.

18. *(b)* I is not true.

A number divisible by 3 and by 9, if the sum of all its digits can be divided by 3 and by 9, respectively.

∴ Statement II is true.

19. *(d)* For 234*65 is divisible by 11.

$$(2 + 4 + 6) - (3 + * + 5) = 0 \text{ or multiple } 11$$
$$\Rightarrow \quad 12 - 8 - * = 0 \Rightarrow 4 - * = 0 \quad \therefore \quad * = 4$$

20. *(b)* Here, number of dots are double in each number of pattern.

$\therefore$ Number of dots in pattern $50 = 50 \times 2 = 100$

21. *(d)* Let x and y be any two whole numbers.

    I. $(x \times y)$ will also be a whole number. Therefore whole numbers are closed under multiplication.

    II. If $x > y$ or $x = y$, then $(x - y)$ is a whole number but if x < y, then x − y cannot be whole number.

    So, whole numbers are not closed under subtraction.

    III. Since, $x + y = y + x$, therefore the commutative property is true under addition for whole numbers.

    IV. Since, $x + y \neq y + x$, therefore the commutative property is not true under division for whole numbers.

    $\therefore$ The Statement II and IV are not correct.

22. *(c)* Total number of chocolates

$$= 18 \times (12 + 14 + 8)$$
$$= 18 \times 12 + 18 \times 14 + 18 \times 8$$

$\therefore$ We can calculate the total number of chocolates using distributive property of multiplication over addition.

23. *(b)* 8........

Now, consider the smallest numbers 0, 1, 2 and 3.

We get,

8 0 1 2 3........ To be divisible by 9, the sum of the digits should be divisible by 9.

$\therefore$ Consider $8 + 0 + 1 + 2 + 3 + x = 14 + x$

Since, digits should be different.

$$\therefore \qquad\qquad x \neq 1 \quad \Rightarrow \quad x = 4$$

Such that sum of digits $= 14 + 4 = 18$, which is divisible by 9.

So, the required number = 801234

24. *(a)* We know that, if the sum of the digits of a number is divisible by 3, then that number is divisible by 3.

$\therefore$ If a 4-digit number A is divisible by 3, the reverse of the number is also divisible by 3. Hence, the sum of digits will remain the same.

25. *(d)* The smallest three digit number which leaves a remainder 2 when divided by 17

$$= A = 17 \times 6 + 2 = 104$$

and the smallest three digit number which leaves a remainder 7 when divided by $12 = B$

$$= 12 \times 8 + 7 = 103$$
$$\therefore \qquad A + B = 104 + 103 = 207$$

Chapter 3 : Integers

1. *(a)* We know that, negative integers come at the left/below side of 0 (zero) on number line.

$\therefore -3°C$ is the equivalent to 3°C below 0°C.

2. *(d)* 6 points left of 0 means $0 - 6$, then going to 2 points right gives $0 - 6 + 2$.

3. *(b)* Accroding to the number line, $A = 5$

$$B = -10$$
$$C = 20$$
$$\therefore A - (B) + C = 5 - (-10) + 20$$
$$= 5 + 10 + 20 = 35$$

4. *(b)* Height above the ground level is represented by a positive integer always and similarly deposit is also represented by positive integer vice-versa.

Depth between 20 and $42 = 20 - 42 = -22$, that is a negative integer.

$\therefore$ Here, statement (b) represents a negative integer.

5. *(d)* All of the given statements are correct.

6. *(c)* Considering the all options,

(a) $26 - 24 = 2$

(b) $24 - (-29) = 24 + 29 = 53$

(c) $-30 + 31 = 1$

(d) $-2 - 6 = -8$

Hence, option (c) has closest value to O.

7. *(c)* Given,

Sum of two integers $= -35$

One of the integers $= 15$

$\therefore$ Other integer $= -35 - 15 = -50$

8. *(a)* Let a be -5 and b be -8.

i.e., $a > b$

$\therefore b - a = -8 - (-5) = -8 + 5 = -3$

It is negative.

9. *(a)* Minimum temperature at $A = -5°C$

Minimum temperature at $B = -2°C$

We know, $-5 < -2$

$\therefore A$ is cooler than B.

10. *(b)* Change in temperature

$$= -16°C - 10°C$$
$$= -26°C$$

$\therefore$ Temperature falls by $26°C$.

11. *(a)* The largest 5-digit even positive number

$$= 99998$$

The largest 5-digit odd negative number

$$= -10001$$

$\therefore$ Required sum $= 99998 + (-10001)$

$$= 99998 - 10001$$
$$= 89997$$

12. *(d)* Total distance from the roof to the basement floor $= 23 - (-14)$

$$= 23 + 14 = 37 \, \text{ft}$$

13. *(d)* Since, both are above the sea level and are represented by positive integers.

$\therefore$ 650 m and 708 m

14. *(c)* Fund lost in 2010 $= ₹ \, 9000$

Fund lost in 2011 $= ₹ 10000$

Fund lost in 2012 $= ₹ 17000$

Fund gained in 2013 $= ₹ 16000$

Fund gained in 2014 $= ₹ 12000$

$\therefore$ We get the expression $=$

$$-9000 - 10000 - 17000 + 16000 + 12000$$
$$= -8000$$

$$[\because -ve \, \text{sign shows loss}]$$

$\therefore$ Ganesh fund had loss of $₹ \, 8000$.

15. *(d)* Consider

$$2 - [\{1 + (4 - 7) - 8\} - 9]$$
$$= 2 - [\{1 + (-3) - 8\} - 9]$$
$$= 2 - [\{1 - 3 - 8\} - 9]$$

$$= 2 - [\{-10\} - 9]$$
$$= 2 - [-10 - 9]$$
$$= 2 - [-19]$$
$$= 2 + 19 = 21$$

16. *(a)* I. Since, $-7 < -4$

There -7 is on the left side of -4 on the number line. So. I is false.

II. The additive inverse of a negative integer is positive.

e.g. additive inverse of -4 is $+4$.

So, II is true.

III. The integer 5 is located to the right of -4 because $-4 < 5$. So, III is true.

IV. Loss represents negative integer.

$\therefore$ loss of $₹ \, 400$ means $₹ \, (-400)$.

So, IV is true.

17. *(d)* I. <u>Six</u> integers are there between -8 and -1.

II. Every integer less than zero is <u>negative</u>.

III. The successor of predecessor of -30 is <u>-30</u>.

IV. $|(-11) + (-15)| = |-11 - 15| = 26$

and $(11) + (15) = 11 + 15 = 26$

$\therefore \qquad 26 = 26$

V. The additive inverse of zero is <u>zero</u>.

18. *(d)* Largest absolute value with negative sign gives the lowest number.

$\therefore -265$ is the lowest point.

19. *(a)* Point on 25th September $= -265$

Point on 1st October $= -238$

$\therefore$ Difference $= -238 - (-265) = 27$

Hence, increase of 27 points.

20. *(d)* Highest point earned $= 200$

Lowest point earned $= -265$

$\therefore$ Difference $= 200 - (-265) = 465$

Chapter 4 : Fractions

1. *(a)* In figure A, total number of equal parts $= 4$

Shaded parts in figure $A = 2$

So, fraction of shaded parts in figure $A = \dfrac{2}{4} = \dfrac{1}{2}$

Similarly, in figure B, total number of equal parts $= 16$

Shaded parts in figure $B = 8$

So, fraction of shaded parts in figure $B = \dfrac{8}{16} = \dfrac{1}{2}$

$\therefore$ A and B are equivalent fraction.

2. *(d)* Given, $3\dfrac{4}{7} = \dfrac{\square}{14}$

$\Rightarrow \qquad 3\dfrac{4}{7} = \dfrac{3 \times 7 + 4}{7}$

$\qquad\qquad = \dfrac{21 + 4}{7} = \dfrac{25}{7}$

Converting them to equivalent fraction, we get $\dfrac{25}{7} \times \dfrac{2}{2} = \dfrac{50}{14}$

$\therefore \qquad\qquad \square = 50$

3. *(c)* Total number of friends $= 4$

Total number of pancakes $= 5$

$\therefore$ Share of pancake each one get $= \dfrac{5}{4}$

4. *(a)* I. False

II. False, because $13\dfrac{5}{18}$ is a mixed fraction.

III. True

IV. False

5. *(b)* In the given series of fractions, numerator increases adding one and denominators are cube of (numerator + 1).

$\therefore \dfrac{1}{8}, \quad \dfrac{2}{27}, \quad \dfrac{3}{64}, \quad \dfrac{4}{125}, \quad \boxed{\dfrac{5}{216}}, \quad \dfrac{6}{343}$

6. *(a)* If simplest form of two fractions are equal, then the two fractions will be equivalent.

$\therefore$ Simplest form of $\dfrac{7}{20} = \dfrac{7 \times 1}{2 \times 2 \times 5} = \dfrac{7}{20}$

Simplest form of $\dfrac{6}{18} = \dfrac{2 \times 3}{2 \times 3 \times 3} = \dfrac{1}{3}$

Simplest form of $\dfrac{9}{27} = \dfrac{3 \times 3}{3 \times 3 \times 3} = \dfrac{1}{3}$

Simplest form of $\dfrac{17}{51} = \dfrac{17 \times 1}{17 \times 3} = \dfrac{1}{3}$

$\therefore \dfrac{7}{20}$ is not equivalent to $\dfrac{1}{3}$.

7. *(d)*

(i) Given,

$$\dfrac{3}{10} \,\square\, \dfrac{2}{5}$$

Converting them to like fractions, we get

$\dfrac{3 \times 1}{10 \times 1} \,\square\, \dfrac{2 \times 2}{5 \times 2} \Rightarrow \dfrac{3}{10} \,\boxed{<}\, \dfrac{4}{10} \qquad [\because 4 > 3]$

(ii) Given,

$$\dfrac{7}{5} \,\square\, \dfrac{11}{9}$$

Converting them to like fractions, we get

$\dfrac{7 \times 9}{5 \times 9} \,\square\, \dfrac{11 \times 5}{9 \times 5} \Rightarrow \dfrac{63}{45} \,\boxed{>}\, \dfrac{55}{45} \quad [\because 63 > 55]$

8. *(b)* Fraction of shaded parts in figure $A = \dfrac{6}{16}$

And fraction of shaded parts in figure $B = \dfrac{3}{5}$

Comparing both figures A and B,

$\dfrac{6}{16}$ and $\dfrac{3}{5}$

$\Rightarrow \qquad \dfrac{6 \times 5}{16 \times 5}$ and $\dfrac{3 \times 16}{5 \times 16}$

We get, $\quad \dfrac{30}{80} < \dfrac{48}{80}$

$\therefore \qquad\qquad A < B$

9. *(d)* Consider $\dfrac{4}{5}, \dfrac{2}{3}, \dfrac{4}{7}, \dfrac{3}{5}$

Converting them to equivalent fraction, LCM $(5, 3, 7) = 105$

$\therefore$ We get, $\dfrac{84}{105}, \dfrac{70}{105}, \dfrac{60}{105}, \dfrac{63}{105}$

So, descending order is as shown below:

$\dfrac{84}{105} > \dfrac{70}{105} > \dfrac{63}{105} > \dfrac{60}{105}$

$\therefore \qquad \dfrac{4}{5} > \dfrac{2}{3} > \dfrac{3}{5} > \dfrac{4}{7}$

10. *(c)* I. $-\dfrac{5}{3} - \dfrac{1}{3} = -\dfrac{6}{3} = -2$

II. $1\dfrac{2}{9} - \dfrac{1}{6} = \dfrac{1 \times 9 + 2}{9} - \dfrac{1}{6} = \dfrac{11}{9} - \dfrac{1}{6} = \dfrac{22 - 3}{18}$

$\qquad\qquad\qquad [\because \text{LCM of 9 and 6 is 18}]$

$\qquad = \dfrac{19}{18} = 1\dfrac{1}{18}$

III. $\dfrac{17}{3} = 5\dfrac{2}{3}$

IV. $9\dfrac{3}{7} + 4\dfrac{2}{7} = \dfrac{9 \times 7 + 3}{7} + \dfrac{4 \times 7 + 2}{7}$

$\qquad\qquad = \dfrac{66}{7} + \dfrac{30}{7} = \dfrac{96}{7}$

$\qquad\qquad\qquad$ [$\because$ denominators are same]

$\qquad\qquad = 13\dfrac{5}{7}$

11. *(b)* $3\dfrac{1}{5} + 4\dfrac{3}{5}$

$\qquad = \dfrac{3 \times 5 + 1}{5} + \dfrac{4 \times 5 + 3}{5} = \dfrac{16}{5} + \dfrac{23}{5}$

$\qquad = \dfrac{39}{5}$ $\quad$ [$\because$ denominators are same]

$\qquad = 7\dfrac{4}{5}$

12. *(d)* Number of parts shaded in figure I = 6

Total number of parts in figure I $= 15$

$\therefore$ Fraction of parts shaded in figure I $= \dfrac{6}{15}$

Now, number of parts shaded in figure II = 5

Total number of parts in figure II = 9

$\therefore$ Fraction of parts shaded in figure II $= \dfrac{5}{9}$

Now, sum of shaded parts in figures I and II

$\qquad = \dfrac{6}{15} + \dfrac{5}{9} = \dfrac{18 + 25}{45}$

$\qquad\qquad$ [$\because$ LCM of 15 and 9 is 45]

$\qquad = \dfrac{43}{45}$

13. *(c)* $\dfrac{4}{9} + \dfrac{7}{9} + \dfrac{x}{9} = 2\dfrac{1}{9}$

$\Rightarrow \qquad \dfrac{4 + 7}{9} + \dfrac{x}{9} = \dfrac{19}{9}$

$\Rightarrow \quad \dfrac{11}{9} + \dfrac{x}{9} = \dfrac{19}{9} \Rightarrow \dfrac{x}{9} = \dfrac{19}{9} - \dfrac{11}{9}$

$\Rightarrow \qquad \dfrac{x}{9} = \dfrac{19 - 11}{9} \Rightarrow \dfrac{x}{9} = \dfrac{8}{9}$

$\therefore \qquad\qquad x = 8$

14. *(a)* Total number of questions $= 40 + 60 = 100$

Number of questions written = 25

$\therefore$ Fraction of the test written $= \dfrac{25}{100} = \dfrac{1}{4}$

15. *(c)* Number of parts in which chocolate pie is divided $= 17$

Number of parts eaten by Surbhi's friend = 5

Number of parts eaten by Surbhi herself = 3

Number of parts left $= 17 - (5 + 3) = 17 - 8 = 9$

$\therefore$ Fraction of number of parts remained $= \dfrac{9}{17}$

16. *(b)* Part of dish to be served to each guest $= \dfrac{1}{4}$

Number of guests = 32

$\therefore$ Number of dishes she required

$\qquad = \dfrac{1}{4} \times 32 = 8$

17. *(c)* Part of salary used in transport $= \dfrac{3}{12}$

Part of salary used in shopping $= \dfrac{4}{12}$

Total amount used $= \dfrac{3}{12} + \dfrac{4}{12}$

$\qquad\qquad$ [$\because$ LCM of 12 and 12 is 12]

$\qquad = \dfrac{7}{12}$

$\therefore$ Part of salary used in miscellaneous $= 1 - \dfrac{7}{12}$

$\qquad\qquad$ [$\because$ LCM of 1 and 12 is 12]

$\qquad = \dfrac{12 - 7}{12} = \dfrac{5}{12}$

18. *(b)* Number of pieces in each orange $= 10$

Number of pieces in two oranges

$\qquad = 10 \times 2 = 20$

Total number of people = 6

$\therefore$ Share of pieces of oranges each one get

$\qquad = \dfrac{20}{6} = 3\dfrac{2}{6} = 3\dfrac{1}{3}$

19. *(a)* Number of hours Vandana generally works

$\qquad = 12\,\text{h}$

Number of hours she has already worked

$\qquad = 6\dfrac{5}{8} = \dfrac{6 \times 8 + 5}{8} = \dfrac{53}{8}$

$\therefore$ Number of hours she have to work

$\qquad = 12 - \dfrac{53}{8} = \dfrac{96 - 53}{8} = \dfrac{43}{8} = 5\dfrac{3}{8}$

20. *(b)* Fraction of beans in a container having

volume $A = \dfrac{3}{5}$

Fraction of beans in a container having volume thrice of A

$$= \frac{3}{5} \times \frac{1}{3} = \frac{1}{5}$$

21. *(c)* Number of flags made by $\dfrac{2}{5}$ of material

$= 16$

Number of flags made by 1 of material

$$= 16 \times \frac{5}{2}$$

$\therefore$ Number of flags made by $\left(1 - \dfrac{2}{5}\right)$ of

material

$$= 16 \times \frac{5}{2} \times \frac{3}{5} \qquad \left[\because 1 - \frac{2}{5} = \frac{3}{5}\right]$$

$$= 24$$

22. *(a)* Width of one window $= 35$ inches

Number of windows $= 3$

$\therefore$ Total fabric required

$$= 3 \times 35 \times 3\frac{1}{2} = 3 \times 35 \times \frac{7}{2}$$

$$= \frac{735}{2} \text{ inches}$$

23. *(b)* Total dessert left $= \dfrac{3}{5} + \dfrac{4}{7} + \dfrac{5}{8}$

$$= \frac{168 + 160 + 175}{280} = \frac{503}{280} = 1\frac{223}{280}$$

24. *(d)* Diameters of rangolies made by each student are

Saria $= \dfrac{17}{20}$, Mehak $= \dfrac{3}{4}$,

Chetna $= \dfrac{5}{6}$ and Kanika $= \dfrac{7}{10}$

Comparing the given diameters,

$$\frac{17}{20}, \frac{3}{4}, \frac{5}{6}, \frac{7}{10}$$

LCM $(20, 4, 6, 10) = 60$

Now, converting the above fractions into equivalent fractions, we get

$$\frac{51}{60}, \frac{45}{60}, \frac{50}{60}, \frac{42}{60}$$

Now, $\quad \dfrac{42}{60} < \dfrac{45}{60} < \dfrac{50}{60} < \dfrac{51}{60}$

$\therefore \quad \dfrac{7}{10} < \dfrac{3}{4} < \dfrac{5}{6} < \dfrac{17}{20}$

So, $\dfrac{7}{10}$ is the smallest.

$\therefore$ Kanika made the smallest rangoli.

25. *(c)* We know, $A\,@\,B = \dfrac{A + B}{A \times B}$

Then, $12\,@\,8 = \dfrac{12 + 8}{12 \times 8}$

$\therefore \dfrac{12\,@\,8}{8\,@\,4} + \dfrac{10\,@\,6}{6\,@\,2}$

$$= \frac{\left(\dfrac{12+8}{12\times8}\right)}{\left(\dfrac{8+4}{8\times4}\right)} + \frac{\left(\dfrac{10+6}{10\times6}\right)}{\left(\dfrac{6+2}{6\times2}\right)} = \frac{\dfrac{20}{96}}{\dfrac{12}{32}} + \frac{\dfrac{16}{60}}{\dfrac{8}{12}}$$

$$= \frac{20}{96} \times \frac{32}{12} + \frac{16}{60} \times \frac{12}{8}$$

$$= \frac{5}{9} + \frac{2}{5} = \frac{5 \times 5 + 2 \times 9}{45}$$

$$= \frac{25 + 18}{45} = \frac{43}{45}$$

26. *(b)*

(i) Total weight of 5 packets of sugar

$$= 155\frac{1}{5} + 146\frac{1}{3} + 161\frac{1}{2} + 150\frac{1}{4} + 148\frac{1}{6}$$

$$= (155 + 146 + 161 + 150 + 148)$$

$$+ \left(\frac{1}{5} + \frac{1}{3} + \frac{1}{2} + \frac{1}{4} + \frac{1}{6}\right)$$

$$= 760 + \frac{(12 + 20 + 30 + 15 + 10)}{60}$$

[$\because$ LCM of denominators of all fractions is 60]

$$= 760 + \frac{87}{60} = 760 + \frac{29}{20}$$

$$= \frac{760 \times 20 + 29}{20} = \frac{15200 + 29}{20} = \frac{15229}{20} \text{ gm}$$

(ii) Weight of heaviest packet $= 161\dfrac{1}{2}$ gm

Weight of lightest packet $= 146\dfrac{1}{3}$ gm

$$\therefore \text{Required difference} = 161\frac{1}{2} - 146\frac{1}{3}$$

$$= (161 - 146) + \left(\frac{1}{2} - \frac{1}{3}\right)$$

$$= 15 + \frac{3-2}{6} = 15 + \frac{1}{6}$$

$$= \frac{90+1}{6} = \frac{91}{6}\ \text{gm}$$

27. *(b)* Let the length of Crayon Z be A.

According to the question,

$$10\frac{1}{9} = \frac{11\frac{2}{3} + A}{2}$$

$$\Rightarrow \frac{91}{9} \times 2 = \frac{35}{3} + A \Rightarrow A = \frac{182}{9} - \frac{35}{3} = \frac{182-105}{9}$$

$$\Rightarrow \qquad A = \frac{77}{9}\ \text{cm}$$

$\therefore$ Total length of Crayon X, Y and Z

$$= \frac{35}{3} + \frac{91}{9} + \frac{77}{9} = \frac{105+91+77}{9}$$

$$= \frac{273}{9} = \frac{91}{3} = 30\frac{1}{3}\ \text{cm}$$

Chapter 5 : Decimals

1. *(a)* We know, the place value table for decimal number,

Whole Part		Decimal Point	Decimal Part	
Tens	Ones	.	Tenths	Hundredths
10	1	.	$\frac{1}{10}$	$\frac{1}{100}$

$\therefore$ Seven and five hundredths

$$= 7 \times 1 + 0 \times \frac{1}{10} + 5 \times \frac{1}{100} = 7.05$$

2. *(c)* Expanded form of 90.9

$$= 9 \times 10 + 0 \times 1 + 9 \times \frac{1}{10}$$

$$= 90 + \frac{9}{10}$$

So, 90.9 can bewritten 'in words as Ninety and nine tenths.

3. *(c)* Greatest possible decimal fraction upto four decimal places = 0.9999

Hence, option (c) is correct.

4. *(b)* Consider $0.25 = \frac{25}{100} = \frac{1}{4}$

In option figure (b) the total number of shaded parts is equal to 2, whereas total number of parts is 8.

So, fraction of shaded parts $= \frac{2}{8} = \frac{1}{4} = 0.25$

Hence, option (b) is correct.

5. *(c)* Given, $y = \frac{126}{630} = \frac{1}{5} = 0.2$

$\therefore 0.2$ is greater than 0 and less than 1. To representing on number line.

0.2 0.4 0.6 0.8
0 y 1

So, the number line given in option (c) is correct representation of y.

Hence, option (c) is correct.

6. *(c)* From the given number line,

$$P = 0.3, Q = 1.5\ \text{and}\ R = 2.2$$

$$\therefore\ P + Q + R = 0.3 + 1.5 + 2.2 = 4$$

7. *(d)* By observing the tenth place and hundredths place digit, we get

$$0.13 < 0.16 < 0.25 < 0.5$$

Hence, option (d) is correct.

8. *(c)* From options,

(a) $56\% = \frac{56}{100} = 0.56$

So, $0.56 < 0.5$ (not correct)

(b) $0.33 = \frac{33}{100} = \frac{4}{9}$ (not correct)

(c) $36 > \frac{9}{25} \Rightarrow 36 > 0.36$ (correct)

(d) $\frac{1}{7} > 0.186 \Rightarrow 0.142 > 0.186$ (not correct)

Hence, option (c) is correct.

9. *(d)* From statements,

I. 3 hundredths + 3 tenths $= \frac{3}{100} + \frac{3}{10}$

$$= 0.03 + 0.3 = 0.33 \neq 33\ \text{(False)}$$

II. Value of a digit at tenths place is not same as the $\frac{1}{10}$ times the same digit at hundredths place. (False)

III. $17.22 < 17.099$ (False)

IV. 10 coins of 40 paise $= 10 \times 0.40 = ₹ 4 \neq ₹ 40$ (False)

10. *(c)* Given, decimal number $= 7.24$

Then, $7.24 = 7 \times 1 + \dfrac{2}{10} + \dfrac{4}{100}$

$$= \frac{700 + 20 + 4}{100} = \frac{724}{100} = \frac{181}{25} = 7\frac{6}{25}$$

11. *(b)* The expanded form of

$$273.04 = 2 \times 100 + 7 \times 10 + 3 \times 1$$
$$+ \, 0 \times \frac{1}{10} + 4 \times \frac{1}{100}$$
$$= 200 + 70 + 3 + \frac{0}{10} + \frac{4}{100}$$

12. *(b)* Given, $0.090909 = \dfrac{1}{11}$

Multiply by 5 on both sides, we get

$$5 \times 0.090909 = 5 \times \frac{1}{11}$$
$$\therefore \qquad 0.454545 = \frac{5}{11}$$

13. *(c)* Amount of orange juice $= 1.5$ liters

Amount of apple juice $= 1.35$ liters

$\therefore$ Total amount of juice $= 1.5 + 1.35 = 2.85$ liters

14. *(c)* Multiplication of any number by 0 gives 0 in the product.

$$\therefore \qquad 7.2 \times 9.69 \times 0.0 \times 4.2 = 0$$

15. *(b)* Given expression,

$$\frac{(8.5 + 7.8 \times 6.5 + 1.3 - 1)}{(7.5 \times 1.6 + 7.5 \times 0.4)} = \frac{(8.5 + 7.8 \times 5 - 1)}{7.5\,(1.6 + 0.4)}$$

[On applying VBODMAS in numerator and take 7.5 common in denominator]

$$= \frac{(8.5 + 39 - 1)}{7.5 \times 2} = \frac{47.5 - 1}{7.5 \times 2} = \frac{46.5}{7.5 \times 2}$$
$$= \frac{46.5}{15} = 3.1$$

16. *(a)* From statements,

I. 0.8625 lies between 0.86 and 0.863.

II. The fraction $14\dfrac{2}{10} = 14 + \dfrac{2}{10} = 14 + 0.2 = \underline{14.2}$

III. 14.572 correct to the tenths place is 14.6.

IV. The value of 79 kg 9 gm is $= 79 + \dfrac{9}{1000}$

$$\left[\because 1 \text{ gm} = \frac{1}{1000} \text{ kg} \right]$$
$$= 79 + 0.009 = \underline{79.009}\,\text{kg}$$

17. *(d)* Consider 9.009, 0.99, 1.11, 0.09, 0.909, 10.101

We have,

$$10.101 > 9.009 > 1.11 > 0.99 > 0.909 > 0.09$$

Hence, option (d) is correct.

18. *(b)* Total cost of two toys, three pencils and five rubbers $= ₹ 234.50$

Cost of two toys and three pencils
$$= ₹ 210$$

Then, cost of five rubbers
$$= ₹ 234.50 - ₹ 210$$
$$= ₹ 24.50$$

$\therefore$ The cost of one rubber
$$= \frac{24.50}{5} = ₹ 4.90$$

19. *(b)* According to the question,

$$96.2205 = 9 \times 10 + 6 \times 1 + 2 \times \frac{1}{10}$$
$$+ \, 2 \times \frac{1}{100} + 0 \times \frac{1}{1000} + 5 \times \frac{1}{10000}$$
$$= 9 \times A + 6 \times B + 2 \times C + \frac{2}{D} + 5 \times E$$

On comparison,

$$A = 10,\, B = 1,\, C = \frac{1}{10},$$
$$D = 100,\, E = \frac{1}{10000}$$

$\therefore$ The value of $4A + 5B + 2C + D + \dfrac{7}{E}$

$$= 4 \times 10 + 5 \times 1 + 2 \times \frac{1}{10} + 100 + \frac{7}{\dfrac{1}{10000}}$$
$$= 40 + 5 + \frac{2}{10} + 100 + 70000$$
$$= 70145.2$$

Chapter 6 : Ratio and Proportion

1. (a) Converting the all ratio in simplest form, we get

$$\frac{9}{12} = \frac{3 \times 3}{3 \times 4} = \frac{3}{4}$$

$$\frac{14}{10} = \frac{2 \times 7}{2 \times 5} = \frac{7}{5},$$

$$\frac{28}{20} = \frac{4 \times 7}{4 \times 5} = \frac{7}{5},$$

and $$\frac{21}{15} = \frac{3 \times 7}{3 \times 5} = \frac{7}{5}$$

Here, the simplest form of all ratio is equal except 9 : 12.

So, 9 : 12 is odd one.

2. (c) Given, $a : b = 2 : 3$

and $b : c = 5 : 7$

$$\frac{a}{b} = \frac{2}{3} = \frac{2 \times 5}{3 \times 5} = \frac{10}{15}$$

and $$\frac{b}{c} = \frac{5 \times 3}{7 \times 3} = \frac{15}{21}$$

∴ $a : b : c = 10 : 15 : 21$

3. (b) Required ratio $= \left(\frac{1}{4} \text{ of } 12.40\right) : (0.8 \text{ of } 1.35)$

$$= \left(\frac{1}{4} \times 12.40\right) : (0.8 \times 1.35) = 3.1 : 1.08$$

$$= \frac{3.1}{1.08} = \frac{310}{108} = \frac{155}{54}$$

4. (a) Total number of matches played $= 30$

Number of matches won $= 12$

Number of matches lost $= 30 - 12 = 18$

∴ Required ratio $= \frac{30}{18} = \frac{5}{3} = 5 : 3$

5. (b) Number of shaded parts

$$= \frac{1}{2} + \frac{1}{2} + \frac{1}{2} + \frac{1}{2} + \frac{1}{2} + \frac{1}{2} + 1$$

$$= 3 + 1 = 4$$

Number of unshaded parts $= 20 - 4 = 16$

∴ Required ratio $= \frac{4}{16} = \frac{1}{4}$

6. (c) Given ratio $= \frac{2}{5}$

According to the questions,

$$\frac{2 + x}{5 + x} = \frac{5}{6}$$

⇒ $12 + 6x = 25 + 5x$

∴ $x = 13$

7. (b) Given,

$$\frac{4}{15}x = \frac{2}{5}y$$

⇒ $$\frac{x}{y} = \frac{2}{5} \times \frac{15}{4}$$

⇒ $$\frac{x}{y} = \frac{3}{2}$$

∴ $$\frac{x + y}{x - y} = \frac{\left(\frac{x}{y}\right) + 1}{\left(\frac{x}{y}\right) - 1} = \frac{\frac{3}{2} + 1}{\frac{3}{2} - 1} = \frac{3 + 2}{3 - 2} = 5$$

8. (c) According to the question,

Total time spent by students at school

$= 1 : 00 \text{ pm} - 7 : 30 \text{ am}$

$= 5 \text{ h } 30 \text{ min} = [(5 \times 60) + 30] \text{ min} = 330 \text{ min}$

Total break time $= 15 \text{ min} + 25 \text{ min} = 40 \text{ min}$

∴ Required ratio $= \frac{40}{330} = \frac{4}{33} = 4 : 33$

9. (b) Given, $64 : 32 = 8 : x$

⇒ $$\frac{64}{32} = \frac{8}{x}$$

∴ $$x = \frac{8 \times 32}{64} = 4$$

10. (d) Mean proportional between a and $b = \sqrt{ab}$.

11. (b) Let fourth proportional be x.

Then, $3 : 5 :: 18 : x$

⇒ $$\frac{3}{5} = \frac{18}{x}$$

⇒ $$x = \frac{18 \times 5}{3}$$ ∴ $x = 30$

12. (c) Given, 8, 16 and 32 are in continued proportion. Here, 16 is called the mean proportion and 32 is called the third proportion.

∴ Required sum $= 16 + 32 = 48$

13. *(d)* Cost of 5 tickets $= ₹60$

Then, cost of 1 ticket $= \dfrac{60}{5} = ₹\,12$

$\therefore$ Cost of 12 tickets $= 12 \times 12 = ₹144$

14. *(a)* Earning of Gaika $= ₹\,24000$

Money spent on rent $= \dfrac{2}{5} \times 24000 = ₹\,9600$

Money spent on food $= ₹\,3600$

$\therefore$ Required ratio $= 3600 : 9600 = 3 : 8$

15. *(a)* Work done in 24 days by $= 14$ men

Work done in 1 day by $= (14 \times 24)$ men

$\therefore$ Work done in 16 days by $= \left(\dfrac{14 \times 24}{16} \right)$ men

$$= 21 \text{ men}$$

16. *(d)* Let length and breadth of a rectangle be $7x$ cm and $6x$ cm respectively.

Given, semi-perimeter $= 117$ cm

$\Rightarrow \qquad (7x + 6x) = 117$

$\Rightarrow \qquad\qquad 13x = 117$

$\Rightarrow \qquad\qquad\quad x = 9$

$\therefore$ Area of rectangle $= l \times b$

$$= 7x \times 6x$$
$$= 7 \times 9 \times 6 \times 9$$
$$= 3402 \text{ sq units}$$

17. *(a)* Let the height of Lipika $= x$ cm

Then, height of Komal $= (40 + x)$ cm.

According to the question,

$$\dfrac{40 + x}{x} = \dfrac{7}{5}$$

$$200 + 5x = 7x$$

$\Rightarrow \qquad\qquad 200 = 2x$

$\Rightarrow \qquad\qquad\quad x = 100$

$\therefore$ Height of Komal $= 100 + 40$

$$= 140 \text{ cm}$$

18. *(c)* Cost of 1 item $= ₹525$

Cost of 50 such items $= ₹(525 \times 50)$

New cost of 1 item $= ₹525 + ₹100 = ₹625$

$\therefore$ Number of item can be bought

$$= \dfrac{525 \times 50}{625} = 42$$

19. *(b)* Let money received by Raghav, Vandana and Eva be $10x$, $9x$ and $7x$ respectively.

Total money $= ₹\,520$

According to the question,

$$10x + 9x + 7x = 520$$

$\Rightarrow \qquad\qquad 26x = 520$

$\Rightarrow \qquad\qquad\quad x = 20$

$\therefore$ Money received by Vandana $= 9x = 9 \times 20$

$$= ₹\,180$$

20. *(d)* Number of boys : Number of girls

$$= 6 : 7$$

Let number of boys $= 6x$

and number of girls $= 7x$

Given, $\dfrac{2}{3}$ of boys leave the auditorium.

$\therefore$ Number of boys $= 6x - \dfrac{2}{3} \times 6x$

$$= 6x - 4x = 2x$$

According to the question,

$$7x - 2x = 70$$

$\Rightarrow \qquad\qquad 5x = 70$

$\Rightarrow \qquad\qquad\quad x = 14$

So, number of students $= 6x + 7x$

$$= 13x = 13 \times 14$$
$$= 182$$

21. *(d)* Let the donation given by Manoj to an old age home $= ₹\,5x$

and the donation given by Manoj to an orphanage $= ₹\,4x$

According to the question,

$$5x + 4x = 72000$$

$\Rightarrow \qquad\qquad 9x = 72000$

$\Rightarrow \qquad\qquad\quad x = \dfrac{72000}{9} = 8000$

$\therefore$ Donation given to an old age home

$$= 5x = 5 \times 8000$$
$$= ₹\,40000$$

Donation given to an orphanage

$$= 4x = 4 \times 8000 = ₹\,32000$$

$\therefore$ Required difference

$$= 40000 - 32000 = ₹\,8000$$

22. *(c)* Given, $A = \dfrac{2}{3}B$

$\Rightarrow$ $3A = 2B$ …(i)

and $B = \dfrac{1}{4}C$

$\Rightarrow$ $4B = C$

Now, $C = 4B = 2(2B)$

$= 2(3A) = 6A$ [From Eq. (i)]

$\therefore$ According to the question,

$A + B + C = 1190$

$\Rightarrow$ $\dfrac{C}{6} + \dfrac{C}{4} + C = 1190$

$\Rightarrow$ $\dfrac{2C + 3C + 12C}{12} = 1190$

$\Rightarrow$ $\dfrac{17}{12}C = 1190$

$\Rightarrow$ $C = ₹\,840$

$\therefore$ A' share $= \dfrac{840}{6} = ₹\,140$

and B' share $= \dfrac{840}{4} = ₹210$

23. *(a)* Let length and breadth of the field be $5x$ cm and $2x$ cm respectively.

(i) Length $= 20$ cm   [Given]

Then, $5x = 20$

$\Rightarrow$ $x = \dfrac{20}{5} \Rightarrow x = 4$

$\therefore$ Breadth $= C = 2x = 2 \times 4 = 8$ cm

So, perimeter $= E = 2(\text{Length} + \text{Breadth})$

$= 2(20 + 8) = 2 \times 28 = 56$ cm

(ii) Now, breadth $= 12$ cm

$\Rightarrow$ $2x = 12 \Rightarrow x = 6$

Length $= A = 5x = 5 \times 6 = 30$ cm

So, perimeter $= F = 2(\text{Length} + \text{Breadth})$

$= 2(30 + 12) = 2 \times 42$

$= 84$ cm

(iii) Perimeter $= 70$ cm

$\Rightarrow$ $2(5x + 2x) = 70$

$\Rightarrow$ $14x = 70$

$\Rightarrow$ $x = 5$

$\therefore$ Length (B) $= 5x = 5 \times 5 = 25$ cm

Breadth (D) $= 2x = 10$ cm

Now, value of $\dfrac{F + D - E + B - C}{A - D}$

$= \dfrac{84 + 10 - 56 + 25 - 8}{30 - 10} = \dfrac{55}{20}$

$= 2.75$

Chapter 7 : Algebra

1. *(d)* We know that, letters are used to represent variable, therefore x is not a constant.
We know that, value of a constant is fixed so, 2 is a constant.
$\therefore$ None of the above is correct.

2. *(d)* We know that, letters are used to represent variables. Here, in equation B and D , variables x and y are present respectively.
$\therefore$ Both B and D are equations with a variable.

3. *(b)* $4u + 13t - 10u + 5t$

$= 4u - 10u + 13t + 5t = -6u + 18t$

$\therefore$ Coefficient of $u = -6$.

4. *(b)* Given, $14\left(\dfrac{a}{2} - 2\right) + 4 = \dfrac{4}{a} + 9$

$\Rightarrow$ $\dfrac{14a}{2} - 28 + 4 = \dfrac{4}{a} + 9$

$\Rightarrow$ $\dfrac{14a}{2} - \dfrac{4}{a} = 28 + 9 - 4$

$\Rightarrow$ $\dfrac{14a^2 - 8}{2a} = 33$

$\Rightarrow$ $14a^2 - 66a - 8 = 0$

$\therefore$ Here variable is a and its highest exponent (power) is 2.
$\therefore$ Degree of the equation $= 2$

5. *(a)* Let the number be x.
According to the question,

$3x - 12 = 27$

$\Rightarrow$ $3x = 27 + 12$

$\Rightarrow$ $3x = 39$

$\therefore$ $x = \dfrac{39}{3} = 13$

6. *(d)* $\dfrac{7y - 2}{5} = \dfrac{7 \times 6 - 2}{5}$ [$\because y = 6$]

$= \dfrac{42 - 2}{5} = \dfrac{40}{5} = 8$

7. *(b)* Let x be the percent.

Then, $\quad \dfrac{10}{24} \times 100 = x$

$\Rightarrow \quad \dfrac{10}{24} = \dfrac{x}{100}$

Hence, option (b) is correct.

8. *(c)* Let the number of jeans be x.

Then, number of t-shirts bought $= 7x$

Total number of clothes bought
$$= x + 7x = 8x$$

$\therefore$ It should be a multiple of 8 and 46 is not a multiple of 8.

9. *(c)* Andrew weight $= (x + 3)$ kg

Catherin weight $= (x + 3) - 2$
$$= (x + 1) \text{ kg}$$

Bendrick weight $= (x + 1) + 1 = (x + 2)$ kg

$\therefore$ Total of their weights $= x + 3 + x + 1 + x + 2$
$$= (3x + 6) \text{ kg}$$

10. *(b)* Age of Monika $= 24p$ yr

Age of Ben $= \dfrac{24p}{3} = 8p$ yr

Age of Monika, 4 yr ago $= (24p - 4)$ yr

and age of Ben, 4 yr ago $= (8p - 4)$ yr

So, total of their ages $= 24p - 4 + 8p - 4$
$$= (32p - 8) \text{ yr}$$

11. *(a)* According to the question, Algebraic expression

$$= \left(y \times \dfrac{1}{b} \right) - \left(x \times \dfrac{1}{a} \right)$$

$$= \dfrac{y}{b} - \dfrac{x}{a} = -\left(\dfrac{x}{a} - \dfrac{y}{b} \right)$$

12. *(a)* Given,

$$5x - 2(7x + 1) = 14x$$
$$\Rightarrow \quad 5x - 14x - 2 = 14x$$
$$\Rightarrow \quad -9x - 2 = 14x$$

13. *(c)* Consider

$$7x - [3y - \{4x - (5z - 3y)$$
$$+ 6z - 3(2x + y - 3z)\}]$$
$$= 7x - [3y - \{4x - 5z + 3y$$
$$+ 6z - 6x - 3y + 9z\}]$$

$$= 7x - [3y - \{-2x + 10z\}]$$
$$= 7x - [3y + 2x - 10z]$$
$$= 7x - 3y - 2x + 10z = 5x - 3y + 10z$$

14. *(d)* $\dfrac{3}{4}P - 3\dfrac{1}{3} = 4\dfrac{1}{3}$

$$\Rightarrow \quad \dfrac{3}{4}P - \dfrac{10}{3} = \dfrac{13}{3}$$

$$\Rightarrow \quad \dfrac{3}{4}P = \dfrac{13}{3} + \dfrac{10}{3}$$

$$\Rightarrow \quad \dfrac{3}{4}P = \dfrac{23}{3}$$

$$\Rightarrow \quad P = \dfrac{23}{3} \times \dfrac{4}{3} \quad \therefore \quad P = \dfrac{92}{9}$$

15. *(b)* Let the three numbers be x, y and z.

Then, sum of these numbers $= x + y + z$

Sum of their reciprocals $= \dfrac{1}{x} + \dfrac{1}{y} + \dfrac{1}{z}$

$\therefore$ Required product
$$= (x + y + z) \times \left(\dfrac{1}{x} + \dfrac{1}{y} + \dfrac{1}{z} \right)$$

16. *(c)* Total amount $= ₹\ x$

Total amount is equally divided among 3 childrens.

Then, initial amount of her daughter $= ₹\ \dfrac{x}{3}$

Amount spent by her daughter $= 3 \times 30 = ₹\ 90$

$\therefore$ Left amount with her $= ₹\left(\dfrac{x}{3} - 90 \right)$

17. *(a)* In triangle let the other side be x units.

$\therefore$ Length of smallest side $= x - 5$

and length of largest side $= 2x + 2$

$\therefore$ Perimeter of the triangle
$$= \text{Sum of lengths of all sides}$$
$$= 2x + 2 + x + x - 5$$
$$= 4x - 3 \text{ units}$$

18. *(b)* Given, $\quad C = 120 + 20n \quad$ and $\quad C = 360$

$\therefore$ We have,
$$360 = 120 + 20n$$
$$\Rightarrow \quad 360 - 120 = 20n$$
$$\Rightarrow \quad 240 = 20n$$
$$\Rightarrow \quad \dfrac{240}{20} = n \Rightarrow 12 = n$$

19. *(c)* Let the number of blue and red pens be $2x$ and $3x$.

∴ We have,

$$2x + 3x = 25$$
$$\Rightarrow \quad 5x = 25$$
$$\therefore \quad x = 5$$

So, numbers of blue and red pens are 2×5 i.e. 10 and 3×5 i.e. 15, respectively.

20. *(d)*

I. 9 more than 5 times the number $x = \underline{5x + 9}$

II. $x = \underline{4}$ is a solution of the equation $7 - x = 3$, because $x = 7 - 3 = 4$

III. An expression with a variable, constant and the sign of equality is called an <u>equation</u>.

IV. The time taken to cover a distance of 20 km at a speed of r km/h is $\dfrac{20}{r}$.

$$\left[\because \text{Time} = \frac{\text{distance}}{\text{speed}} \right]$$

21. *(a)* Given, length of rectangle $ABCD = 4x + 2$

breadth of rectangle $ABCD = 3x + 1$
According to the question,
New length $= 4x + 2 + 3x = 7x + 2$
New breadth $= 3x + 1 - x = 2x + 1$
∴ New perimeter $= 2$ (length + breadth)

$$= 2(7x + 2 + 2x + 1)$$
$$= 2(9x + 3) = 18x + 6$$

22. *(b)* Given, Number of females $= x$

∴ Number of males $= \dfrac{x}{2}$

After an hour, number of females visited $= 2x$ and number of males visited $= 60$

∴ Number of peoples in the restaurant

$$= x + \frac{x}{2} + 2x + 60 = 3x + \frac{x}{2} + 60$$
$$= \frac{6x + x}{2} + 60 = \frac{7x}{2} + 60$$

23. *(c)* Only step-3 is wrong.

Correct step will be that subtract 24 to both sides gives

$$3x + 24 - 24 = 30 - 24$$
$$3x = 6$$

24. *(a)* **From Statement I**

Let the number be x,

∴ According to the question,

$$\left(\frac{x}{2} + \frac{x}{3} + \frac{x}{4} \right) - \frac{3x}{4} = 30$$
$$\Rightarrow \quad \left(\frac{6x + 4x + 3x}{12} \right) - \frac{3x}{4} = 30$$
$$\Rightarrow \quad \frac{13x}{12} - \frac{3x}{4} = 30$$
$$\Rightarrow \quad \frac{13x - 9x}{12} = 30 \quad \Rightarrow \quad x = 90$$

∴ Statement I is true.

From Statement II

Sum of y and $4y = y + 4y = 5y$
We know, greatest two digit number $= 99$
∴ Required difference $= 99 - 5y$
∴ Statement II is false.

Chapter 8 : Elementary Shapes

1. *(d)* $28°, 100°, 90°, 180°$ and $210°$ are acute, obtuse, right, straight and reflex angle respectively.

2. *(a)* We know, an angle which is more than $180°$ but less than $360°$, is called a reflex angle.
∴ In option figure (a) , $\angle AOB > 180°$ but $\angle AOB < 360°$.
So, it is a reflex angle.

3. *(b)* An angle greater than $90°$ and less than $180°$ is called an obtuse angle.
∴ There are 3 obtuse angles, they are $\angle COA$, $\angle DOA$ and $\angle EOB$.

4. *(b)* We know that, if sum of two angles is $180°$, then they are said to be supplementary angles.
∴ Sum of $115° + 65° = 180°$, therefore they are supplementary angles.

5. *(b)* $2\dfrac{1}{3}$ of right angle $= \dfrac{7}{3} \times 90° = 210°$

6. *(d)* Let the angle be $x°$.

Supplement of angle $x = 180° - x$

Complement of angle $x = 90° - x$

According to the question,

$$(180° - x) = 4(90° - x)$$
$$180° - x = 360° - 4x$$
$$\Rightarrow \quad 4x - x = 360° - 180°$$
$$\Rightarrow \quad 3x = 180° \Rightarrow x = \frac{180°}{3} = 60°$$

7. *(b)* Angle between a pair of two consecutive

$$\text{spokes} = \frac{\text{Complete angle}}{\text{Number of spokes}}$$

$$= \frac{360°}{50} = 7\frac{1}{5}°$$

8. *(d)* Since, sum of supplementary angles is $180°$.

$$\therefore \text{ Ist angle} = \frac{4}{4 + 5} \times 180°$$

$$= \frac{4}{9} \times 180° = 80°$$

and IInd angle $= \dfrac{5}{4 + 5} \times 180°$

$$= \frac{5}{9} \times 180° = 100°$$

9. *(b)* Angles which are less than $90°$ are called acute angles, therefore all angles are acute angles.

10. *(c)* We know that, a triangle having no two sides equal, is called a scalene triangle.

$\therefore$ A scalene triangle can <u>sometimes</u> be a right triangle.

11. *(d)* Triangle which has 3 sides of equal length is called an <u>Equilateral triangle</u>.

Triangle which has two sides of equal length is called an <u>Isosceles triangle</u>.

Triangle which has one right angle with two sides of equal length is called <u>Isosceles right angled triangle</u>.

Triangle which has all sides are of different length is called <u>scalene triangle</u>.

12. *(c)* $360°$ angle $= 1$ complete turns

$$\therefore \ 180° \text{ angle} = \frac{1}{360°} \times 180° \text{ complete turns}$$

$$= \frac{1}{2} \text{ turns}$$

13. *(d)* Given,

Angle made by minute hand in 1 min $= 6°$

$\therefore$ Angle made by minute hand in 20 min

$$= 6° \times 20 = 120°$$

14. *(a)* Time $6:50$ in a clock,

We know that, angle made by minute hand in 1 min is $6°$ and angle made by hour hand in 1 min is $\dfrac{1°}{2}$ or in 1 h is $30°$.

$\therefore$ Angle is formed between the two hands at

$$6:50 = 50 \times 6° - \left(30 \times 6° + 50 \times \frac{1°}{2} \right)$$

$$= 300° - (180° + 25°)$$

$$= 95°, \text{ it is an obtuse angle}$$

15. *(c)* There are 16 right angles, those are $\angle DHF$, $\angle DEO$, $\angle OEA$, $\angle EAF$, $\angle AFO$, $\angle OFB$, $\angle FBG$, $\angle BGO$, $\angle OGC$, $\angle GCH$, $\angle CHO$, $\angle OHD$, $\angle HOG$, $\angle HOE$, $\angle GOF$ and $\angle EOF$.

16. *(a)* We know that, if all sides are equal and all the angles are $90°$ of a quadrilateral, then the quadrilateral is called a <u>square</u>.

17. *(b)* We know that, opposite angles are equal in a parallelogram.

$\therefore \qquad\qquad y = 120°$

and $x = 60°$

18. *(b)* We know that, sum of all interior angles of a quadrilateral is $360°$.

In given quadrilateral $ABCD$,

$$108° + y + 76° + 65° = 360°$$
$$\Rightarrow \quad y = 360° - (108° + 76° + 65°) = 360° - 249°$$
$$\therefore \quad y = 111°$$

19. *(c)* In $\triangle ABC$, $70° + 60° + 30° + x = 180°$

       [Sum of angle of a triangle is $180°$]
$$\Rightarrow \qquad 160° + x = 180°$$
$$\Rightarrow \qquad x = 180° - 160° = 20°$$

Now, In $\triangle ABD$,

$$60° + 20° + 70° + y = 180°$$

       [Sum of angle of a triangle is $180°$.]
$$\therefore \qquad y = 180° - 150° = 30°$$

20. *(a)* A cuboid with all the edges of same length is called a <u>cube</u>.

21. *(c)* A sphere has only 1 curved face.

22. *(d)* A. The term which is associated with an edge of your book is a <u>line segment</u>.

B. The angle formed at each corner of an envelope is <u>right angle</u>.

C. Angle formed by minute hand in 10 min
$$= 10 \times 6° = 60°$$

D. Given, five-sixth of a right angle
$$= \frac{5}{6} \times 90° = 75°$$

$\therefore$ Supplement of $75° = 180° - 75° = 105°$

E. In one angle of a triangle is equal to the sum of the other two equal angles, then the triangle is a <u>right triangle</u>.

F. Let the angle be 'x'.

Given, $(180° - x) - x = 46°$
$$\Rightarrow 180° - 46° = 2x \Rightarrow x = \frac{134°}{2} = 67°$$

$\therefore$ Supplement of $67° = 180° - 67° = 113°$

So, A $\rightarrow$ (r), B $\rightarrow$ (s), C $\rightarrow$ (t), D $\rightarrow$ (u),

     E $\rightarrow$ (p), F $\rightarrow$ (q)

23. *(d)* From $\triangle ABD$,

$$60° + 60° + x = 180° \quad [\because \text{Angle sum property}]$$
$$\Rightarrow \quad x = 180° - 120° = 60°$$

and $y = 60° + 60°$ $[\because$ Exterior angle property]
$$y = 120°$$

From $\triangle ADC$, $20° + y + z = 180°$

         [$\because$ Angle sum property]

$$\Rightarrow \quad 20° + 120° + z = 180°$$
$$\Rightarrow \quad z = 180° - 140° = 40°$$
$$\therefore \qquad x + y - z = 60° + 120° - 40° = 140°$$

24. *(b)* We know that, in a triangular prism,

     Face = 5,

   Vertices $= X = 6,$

    Edges = 9

In a square pyramid, Face = 5,

Vertices = 5,

    Edges $= Y = 8$

and in a pentagonal prism, Face = 7,

Vertices $= Z = 10$

   Edges $= 15$

$\therefore \quad X + Y - Z = 6 + 8 - 10 = 14 - 10 = 4$

Chapter 9 : Geometry

1. *(b)* A line has no end points.

So, the statement (b) is false.

2. *(c)*

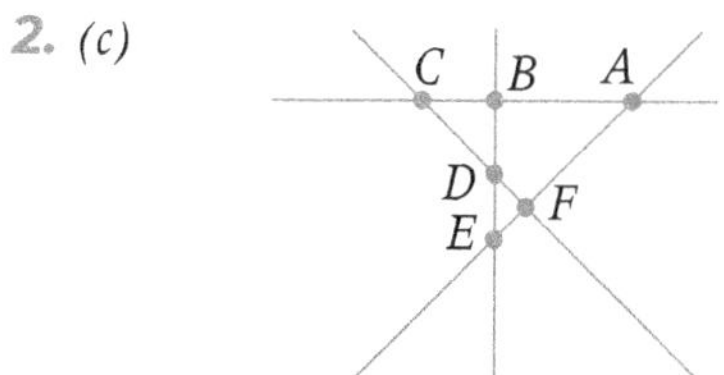

A, B, C, D, E and F are the six points in which the lines can intersect.

3. *(b)* The minimum number of lines that must bind a plane figure is 3.

Triangle is the least sided closed figure.

4. *(c)* Length of $PQ = 8.5$ cm

Arc is cut off at R, $PR = 6.2$ cm

$\therefore$ Remaining length
$$= RQ = PQ - PR = 8.5 - 6.2 = 2.3 \text{ cm}$$

5. *(c)* Here, first arc cut off shows $60°$ because arc BD is equal to ar DE.

6. *(d)* We know that, a right angle is $90°$.

$\therefore \angle BOE = 45° + 45° + 45° = 135°$

$\therefore \angle BOA = 45°,$

$\therefore \angle AOE = 45° + 45° + 45° + 45° = 180°$

and $\angle BOD = 45° + 45° = 90°$

$\therefore \angle BOD$ is a right angle.

7. *(c)* Number of turns made = six and a half = 6.5

∴ Number of revolutions = 6.5

Straight angles formed in one revolution = 2

∴ Straight angles formed in 6.5 revolutions
$$= 2 \times 6.5 = 13$$

8. *(c)* Given,

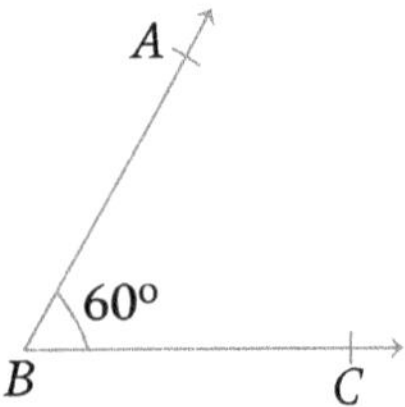

When, we divide angle 60° into five equal angles with the help of compass and ruler.

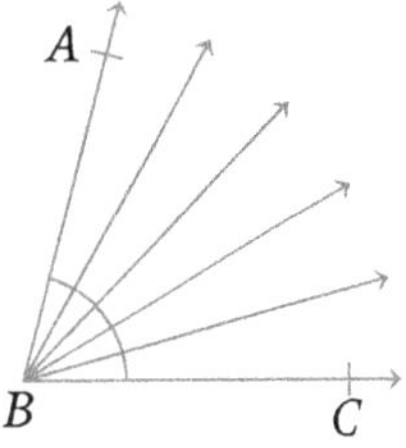

Now, by measuring protractor, each angle would be of $60° \div 5 = 12°$.

9. *(b)* Given,

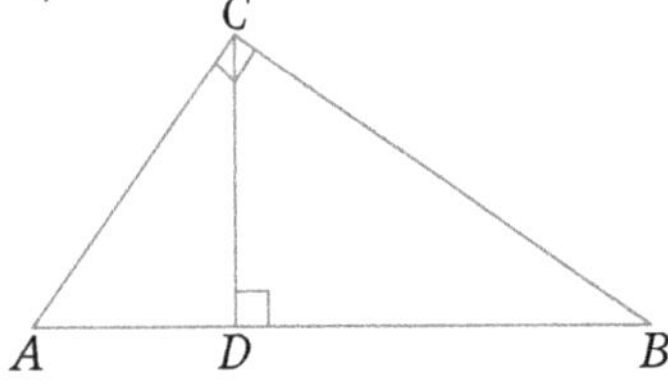

Number of right angle triangle are 3, they are ΔCDB, ΔCDA and ΔACB.

10. *(a)* There are 17 triangles in the given figure,

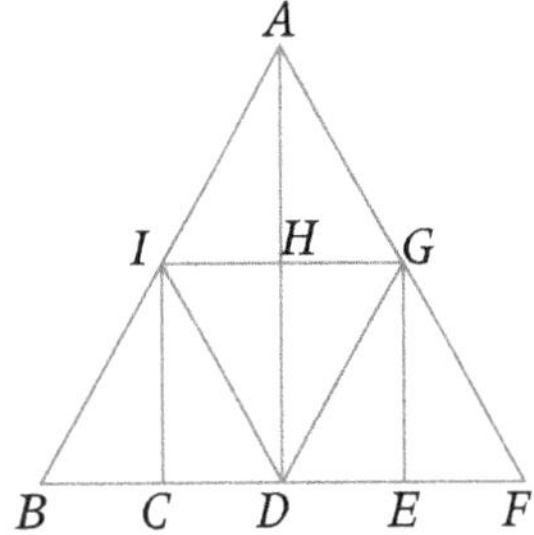

ΔAHI, ΔAHG, ΔAIG, ΔBIC, ΔCID, ΔBID, ΔIDH, ΔHDG, ΔIDG, ΔDGE, ΔFGE, ΔDGF, ΔDGA, ΔDIA, ΔADF, ΔABD and ΔABF.

11. *(b)* $(n - 2)$ triangles can be made in an n sided figure.

∴ Septagon has 7 sides, so $7 - 2 = 5$ triangles.

12. *(a)* Given,

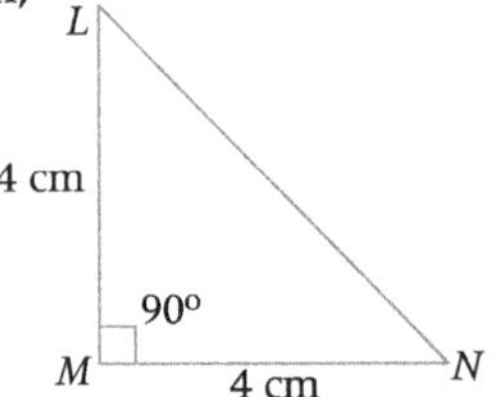

Here, $\angle LMN = 90°$ so, it is a right angle triangle.

$LM = MN = 4$ cm. so, it is an isosceles triangle.

∴ ΔLMN is an isosceles right triangle.

13. *(b)* I. A triangle with sides 2 cm, 1 cm and 4 cm. can not be drawn because we know that, sum of any two sides is greater than the third side, but here $2 + 1 = 3 < 4$.

II. A triangle can not have two obtuse angles.

III. Obviously, a triangle can have all the three acute angles ($< 90°$).

IV. A right triangle has only one angle equal to 90°.

14. *(b)* According to the question,

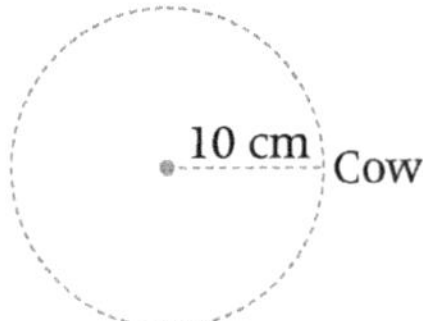

A circle of radius 10 cm is drawn.

15. *(c)* The correct combination is,
A → (3), B → (4), C → (2) and D → (1).

16. *(c)* Number of sides in the given figure is 10. So, it can not be an octagon or quadrilateral. All the sides are not equal, so it can not be a regular polygon.

∴ It is a polygon.

17. *(c)* Number of diagonals in an n sided polygon

$$= \frac{n(n-3)}{2}$$

∴ Number of diagonals in pentagon

$$= \frac{5(5-3)}{2} = \frac{5 \times 2}{2} = 5$$

18. *(c)* The prime number between 5 and 10 is 7.

∴　It is a septagon.

Number of diagonals of a septagon

$$= \frac{n(n-3)}{2} = \frac{7(7-3)}{2}$$

$$= \frac{7 \times 4}{2} = 14$$

19. *(c)* I. A single point has no length, no width.

II. Only one line can be drawn through two points.

III. An octagon has 20 diagonals.

IV. Every chord of circle which passes through the centre of the circle divides it into equal parts.

∴ All the given statements are false.

20. *(c)* When, the base is rectangle and front face looks like triangle, the shape of solid object is rectangular prism.

21. *(c)* Number of diagonals of an n-sided figure

$$= \frac{n(n-3)}{2}$$

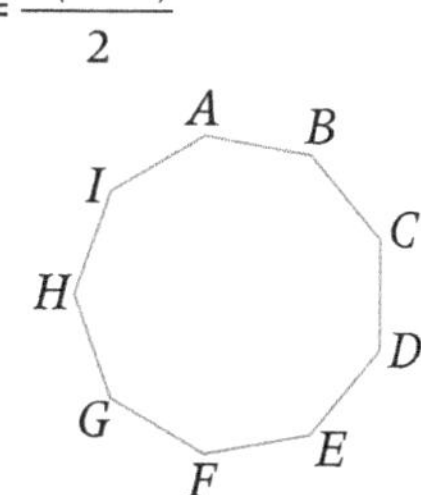

Total number of diagonals = 27

$$27 = \frac{n(n-3)}{2}$$

$\Rightarrow \qquad 27 \times 2 = n(n-3)$

$\Rightarrow \qquad\quad 54 = n^2 - 3n$

$\Rightarrow \quad n^2 - 3n - 54 = 0$

$\Rightarrow \qquad n^2 - 9n + 6n - 54 = 0$

$\Rightarrow \qquad n(n-9) + 6(n-9) = 0$

$\Rightarrow \qquad\quad (n+6)\,(n-9) = 0$

So, $n = 9$ 　　　$\{\because x = -6 \text{ can't be possible}\}$

A polygon having 27 diagonals is a nonagon.

22. *(a)* Since, all angles make a full revolution. So, it is a complete angle.

$(3x - 40)° + (x + 10)° + (3x + 10)°$
$\qquad + (2x + 20)° + (x + 20)° = 360°$

$\Rightarrow \qquad\qquad 10x + 20° = 360°$

$\Rightarrow \qquad\qquad\quad 10x = 340°$

$\Rightarrow \qquad\qquad\qquad x = 34°$

23. *(d)* Since, O is the centre of the given circle.

and $OP = OS = OR$ 　　　[∵ radii of the circle]

∴ 　　　$RS = OR + OS$

$$= 6.4 + 6.4$$

$$= 12.8\ \text{cm}$$

24. *(b)* Since, Q is the centre of the given circle and radius $QA = QO = 5.5$ cm.

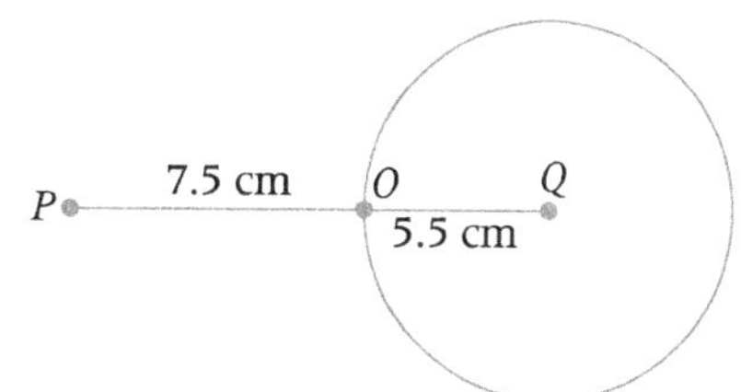

∴ 　　　$QP = PO + OQ$

$$= 7.5 + 5.5 = 13\ \text{cm}.$$

25. *(b)*

I. An angle 0° is called a <u>zero</u> angle.

II. An angle with measure 180° is called a <u>straight</u> angle.

III. The starting point of a ray is called the <u>initial</u> point.

IV. <u>Infinite</u> number of radii can be drawn in a circle.

V. If two lines have one common point, they are called <u>intersecting</u> lines.

Chapter 10 : Symmetry

1. *(b)* Rectangle is not symmetrical about its diagonals.

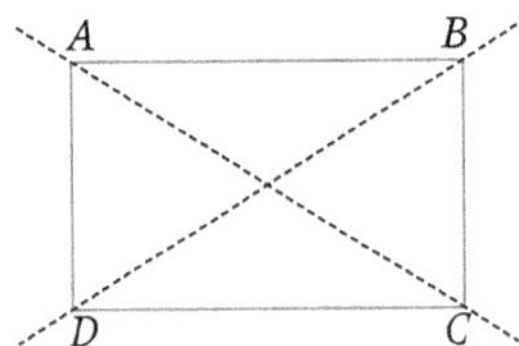

2. *(c)* A regular pentagon has 5 lines of symmetry.

3. *(b)* The number of line of symmetry in a protractor is 1 i.e. vertical line of symmetry.

4. *(a)* The set-square of measurement 30°-60°-90° is in the shape of a scalene right angled triangle and there is no line of symmetry.

∴ The required number of lines of symmetry = 0

5. *(d)*

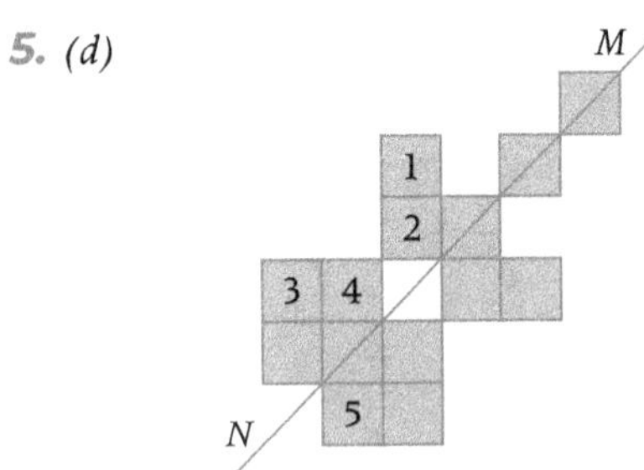

5 squares must be added so that the line *MN* becomes a line of symmetry.

6. *(d)* There is only 1 line of symmetry in the given figure.

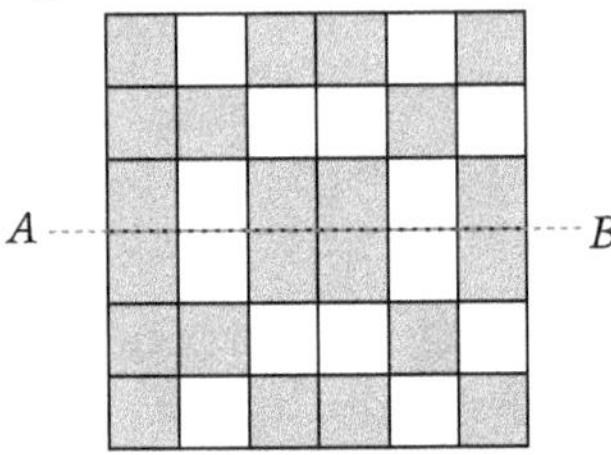

7. *(c)*

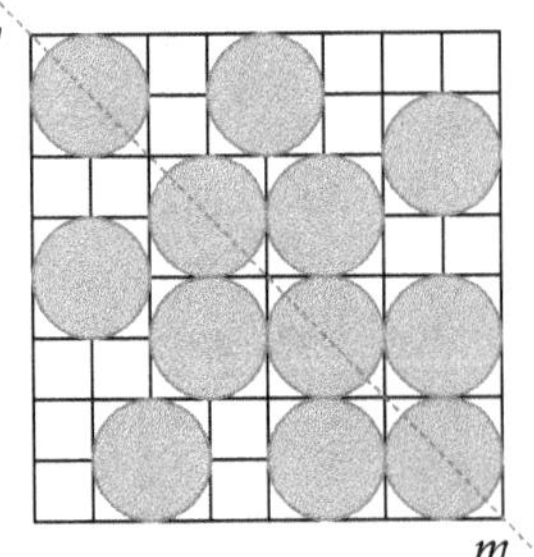

Number of lines of symmetry = 1

8. *(b)* Only figure P and S have atleast one line of symmetry.

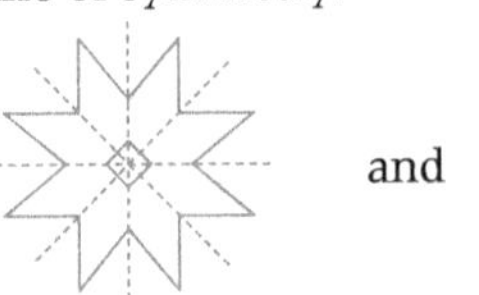 and 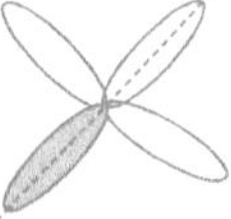

9. *(b)* Only P and S have atleast two lines of symmetry.

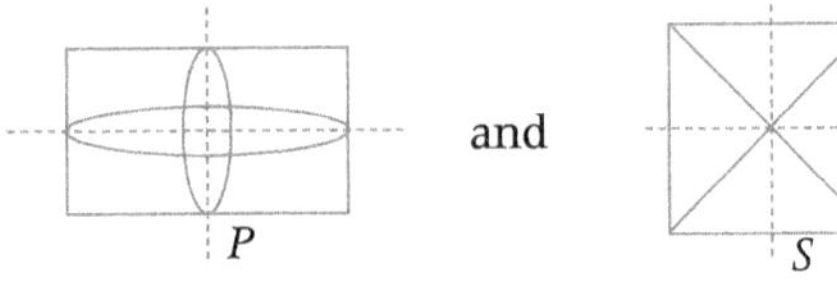

10. *(d)* Only figure d here, has a line of symmetry (i.e., vertical line of symmetry).

11. *(b)* From option (a),

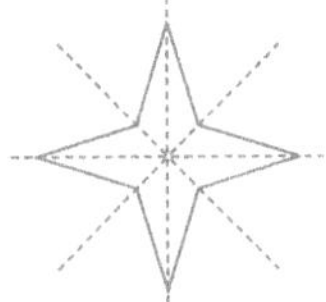

Number of lines of symmetry = 4
From option (b),

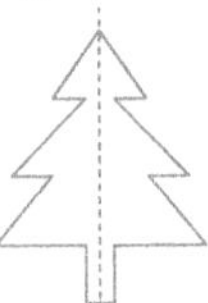

Number of lines of symmetry = 1
From option (c),

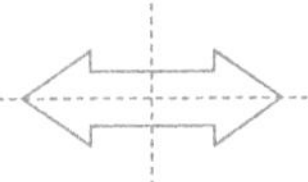

Number of lines of symmetry = 2
From option (d),

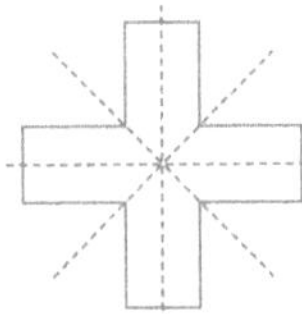

Number of lines of symmetry = 4

12. *(d)* (i)

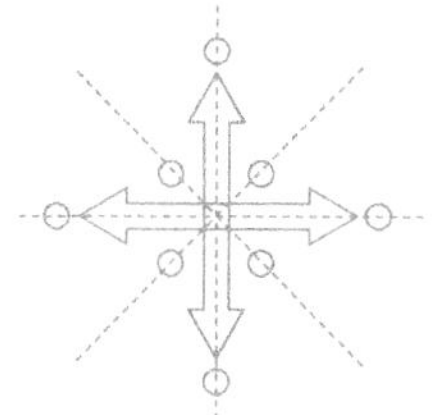

Number of lines of symmetry = 4

(ii)

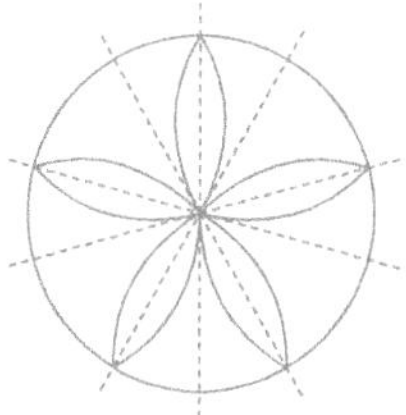

Number of lines of symmetry = 5

13. *(c)* Only alphabet H has both horizontal and vertical line of symmetry.

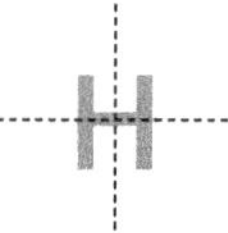

14. *(b)* Only 3 is a digit here, which has exactly one line of symmetry.

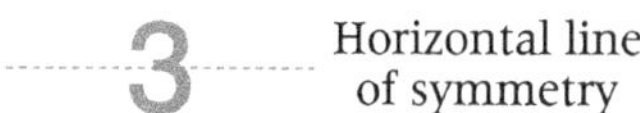

Horizontal line of symmetry

15. *(b)* Here, only letters A and E (i.e. 2 letters) have a line of symmetry.

 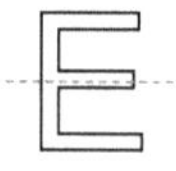

16. *(a)* Minimum 1 square must be shaded to make the given figure symmetrical.

17. *(c)* Least number of squares must be 5 that are added so that the line *MN* becomes a line of symmetry.

18. *(c)* Complete figure with its image from line *l*.

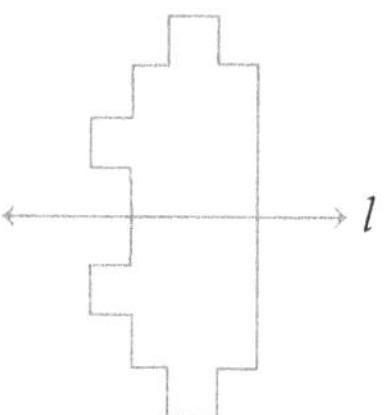

19. *(c)* Only shape (c) is not symmetrical. where as

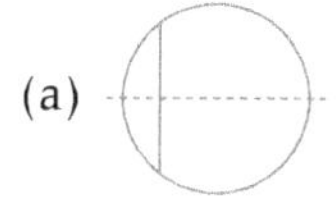 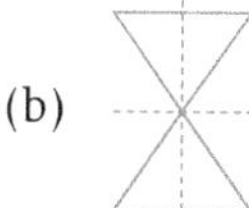 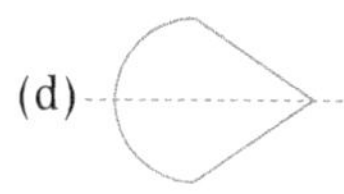

(a)   (b)   (d)

20. *(b)* (i) It is true that each diameter of a circle is an axis of symmetry.

(ii) It is true that a regular polygon has as many lines of symmetry as the number of sides.

(iii) Each one of the letters H, I of English alphabet has atleast two lines of symmetry but M and B has only one line of symmetry.

(iv) It is true that a line segment is symmetrical about its perpendicular bisector.

21. *(c)*

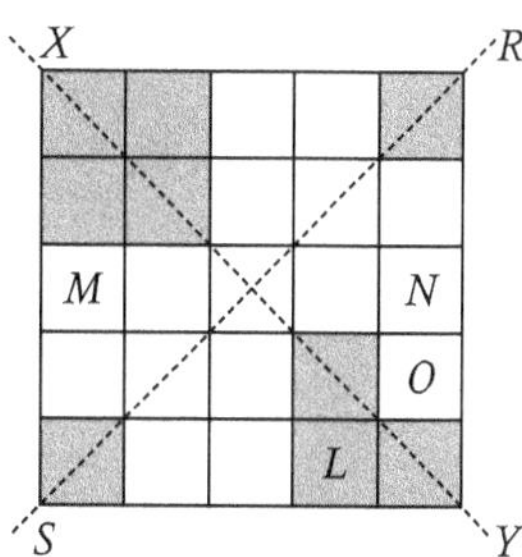

Squares *L* and *O* must be shaded so that the given figure is symmetric along both the lines *XY* and *RS*.

22. *(b)*

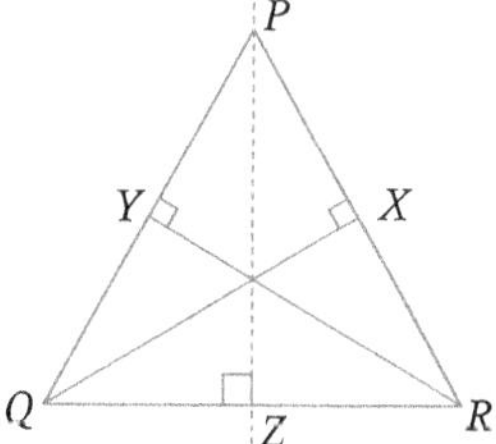

ΔPQR is symmetrical about *PZ*.

23. *(c)* (i) A rhombus has 2 lines of symmetry along its <u>diagonals</u>.

    (ii) All the lines of symmetry of the circle pass through its <u>centre</u>.

    (iii) A right angle triangle may have <u>1</u> line of symmetry.

    (iv) Given alphabet 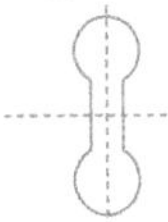 has no line of symmetry.

24. *(a)* Symmetry, of given figures,

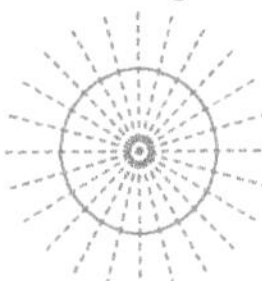

$\therefore$ Number of lines of symmetry $= 2$

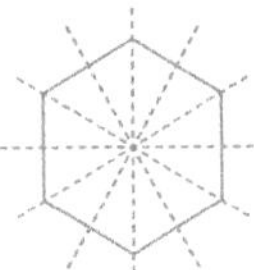

$\therefore$ Number of lines of symmetry $=$ infinite

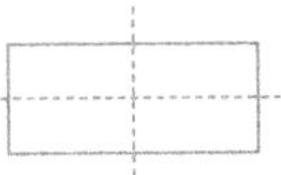

Number of lines of symmetry $= 6$

Number of lines of symmetry $= 2$

$\therefore$ All the 4 figures have atleast two lines of symmetry.

25. *(c)* Reflection figure is (c) of the given figure.

Chapter 11 : Mensuration

1. *(a)* Perimeter of $\triangle ABC = 16 + 18 + 14$

$$= 48\,\text{cm}$$

If this perimeter is used to make a square,

$\therefore$ Side of the square $= \dfrac{48}{4} = 12\,\text{cm}$

2. *(c)* By option (a), Perimeter

$$= 4 \times 3.5 = 14\,\text{cm}$$

By option (b), Perimeter $= 6 + 6 + 2 = 14\,\text{cm}$

By option (c), Perimeter $= 2(6 + 2) = 2 \times 8$

$$= 16\,\text{cm}$$

$\therefore$ Figure (c) has the greatest perimeter.

3. *(d)* Required length of ribbon

$$= \text{Perimeter of window}$$
$$= 2\,(\text{Length} + \text{Breadth})$$
$$= 2(9 + 7) = 2(16) = 32\,\text{m}$$

4. *(c)* Perimeter of the plot $= 2(l + b)$

$$= 2(50 + 40) = 180\,\text{m}$$

$\because$ Stones at a distance of 12 m each.

$\therefore$ Number of stones along the boundary of the plots $= \dfrac{180}{12} = 15$

5. *(d)* Given, length and breadth of the rectangle is 32 m and 16 m respectively.

$\because$ Perimeter of rectangle $= 2(l + b)$

$\therefore$ Perimeter $= 2(32 + 16) = 96\,\text{m}$

Let the side of the equilateral triangle be x m.

$\therefore$ According to the question,

$$3 \times x = 96$$
$$x = \dfrac{96}{3} = 32\,\text{m}$$

6. *(c)* Perimeter of figure (i)

$$= 24 \times 5$$
$$= 120\,\text{cm}$$

Perimeter of figure (ii) $= 36 \times 4 = 144\,\text{cm}$

Perimeter of figure (iii) $= 42 \times 3 = 126\,\text{cm}$

$\therefore$ Perimeter of [(i) + (iii)] > Perimeter of (ii)

$$120 + 126 > 144$$
$$246 > 144$$

7. *(a)* Area of rectangular park $= 2600\,\text{m}^2$

Length $\times$ Breadth $= 2600\,\text{m}^2$

$\Rightarrow$ Length $\times 50 = 2600$

$\Rightarrow$ Length $= \dfrac{2600}{50}$

$$= 52\,\text{m}$$

Distance covered by Rohan in 1 round

$$= 2(52 + 50) = 2 \times 102 = 204\,\text{m}$$

$\therefore$ Distance covered by Rohan in 3 rounds

$$= 204 \times 3 = 612\,\text{m}$$

8. (c) Given, length of rectangular field $= 56\,\text{m}$

Let the breadth of rectangular field be b m.

$$\therefore \qquad l \times b = 2688$$
$$56 \times b = 2688$$
$$\Rightarrow \qquad b = \frac{2688}{56} = 48\,\text{m}$$

Now, perimeter of rectangular field
$$= 2(l + b) = 2 \times (56 + 48)$$
$$= 2 \times 104 = 208\,\text{m}$$

$\therefore$ Total cost of fencing $= 208 \times 35 = ₹\, 7280$

9. (c) Area of the square $=$ Side $\times$ Side
$$= 12\,\text{m} \times 12\,\text{m} = 144\,\text{m}^2$$

Also, area of the rectangle $= 144\,\text{m}^2$

$\therefore$ Length of the rectangle
$$= \frac{\text{Area of rectangle}}{\text{Breadth}} = \frac{144}{3}$$
$$= 48\,\text{m}$$

$\therefore$ Perimeter of the rectangle
$$= 2 \times (\text{Length} + \text{Breadth})$$
$$= 2 \times (48 + 3)\,\text{m}$$
$$= 2 \times 51 = 102\,\text{m}$$

10. (c) Let the breadth of the field $= x$ m

Then, length $= (3x + 4)$ m

Given, perimeter $= 84$ m
$$\Rightarrow \quad 2(x + 3x + 4) = 84$$
$$\Rightarrow \qquad 4x + 4 = 42$$
$$\Rightarrow \quad 4x = 38 \Rightarrow x = 9.5$$

$\therefore$ Length $= (3 \times 9.5 + 4)\,\text{m} = 32.5\,\text{m}$

and Breadth $= 9.5$ m

$\therefore$ Area $=$ Length $\times$ Breadth $= 32.5 \times 9.5$
$$= 308.75\,\text{m}^2 \approx 309\,\text{m}^2$$

11. (b) Given, Hall's length and breadth $= 32$ m

and 18 m respectively.

$\therefore$ Area of hall $= 32 \times 18\,\text{m}^2$

Length and breadth of one tile $= 3$ m and 2 m respectively

$\therefore$ Area of a tile $= 3 \times 2 = 6\,\text{m}^2$

$\therefore$ Number of tiles to floor $= \dfrac{32 \times 18}{3 \times 2} = 96$

12. (c) Length of the hall $= 10.5$ m

Breadth of the hall $= 4.5$ m

Area of the rectangular hall
$$= (\text{Length} \times \text{Breadth})$$
$$= 10.5\,\text{m} \times 4.5\,\text{m} = 47.25$$

Length of side of the square carpet $= 3.5$ m

Area of the square carpet $= 3.5\,\text{m} \times 3.5\,\text{m}$
$$= 12.25\,\text{m}^2$$

$\therefore$ Area of the hall which will not be carpeted
$$= \text{Area of the rectangular hall}$$
$$- \text{Area of the carpet}$$
$$= 47.25\,\text{m}^2 - 12.25\,\text{m}^2 = 35\,\text{m}^2$$

13. (b) Length of the paper before it is folded
$$= 6 + 5 + 5 + 5 + 5 = 26\,\text{cm}$$

Breadth of the paper $= 5$

$\because$ Paper is in shape of rectangle,

Area of the paper $=$ length $\times$ breadth
$$= 26 \times 5 = 130\,\text{cm}^2$$

14. (b) Given figure is the combination of rectangles.

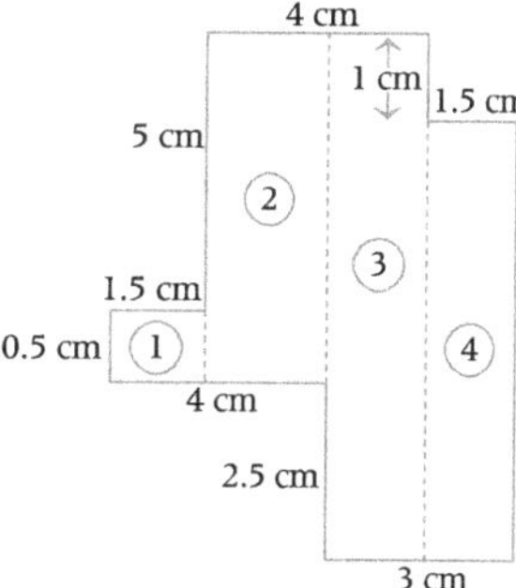

Area of figure $=$ Area of (first $+$ second $+$ third $+$ fourth) figures.
$$= (1.5 \times 0.5) + (5.5 \times 2.5) + (1.5 \times 8) + (1.5 \times 7)$$
$$= 0.75 + 13.75 + 12 + 10.5 = 37\,\text{cm}^2$$

15. (c) Area of rectangle $PQWV = 56$ sq cm
$$\Rightarrow PQ \times QW = 56 \Rightarrow 7 \times QW = 56$$
$$\Rightarrow \qquad QW = 8\,\text{cm}$$

Area of rectangle $VWTU = 42$ sq cm
$$\Rightarrow \qquad VW \times WT = 42$$
$$\Rightarrow \qquad 7 \times WT = 42$$
$$\Rightarrow \qquad WT = 6\,\text{cm}$$

As, $QT = QW + WT = 8 + 6 = 14\,\text{cm}$

Area of rectangle $QRST = 70$ sq cm
$$\Rightarrow QR \times QT = 70 \Rightarrow QR \times 14 = 70$$

$\Rightarrow \qquad QR = 5\text{ cm} = ST$

$\Rightarrow \qquad US = UT + TS = 7 + 5$

$$= 12\text{ cm}$$

16. *(b)* Area of $EFGH$

$$= HG \times GF$$
$$= (169 - 9) \times (169 - 9)$$
$$= 160 \times 160$$
$$= 25600\text{ m}^2$$

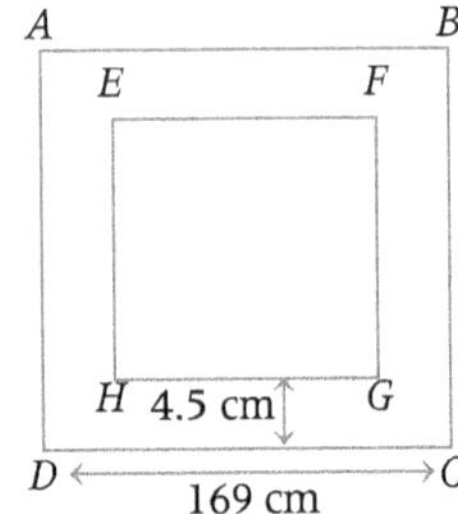

17. *(a)* Given, length of rectangle $ABCD = 30\text{ cm}$

breadth of rectangle $ABCD = \dfrac{30}{3} = 10\text{ cm}$

(A) $\therefore$ Sum of perimeter of rectangle $ABCD$ and
$SNBA = 2 \times (30 + 10) + 2\,(35 + 15)$

$$= 80 + 100 = 180\text{ cm}$$

(B) Area of rectangle $LNCM = 35 \times 15$

$$= 525\text{ cm}^2$$

18. *(c)* Side the largest square $= 12\text{ cm}$

According to the question,

Side of middle square $= \dfrac{12}{2} = 6\text{ cm}.$

and side of smallest square $= \dfrac{6}{2} = 3\text{ cm}.$

(i) $\therefore$ Perimeter of the figure
$$= 12 + 6 + 6 + 3 + 3 + 3 + 21 + 12$$
$$= 66\text{ cm}$$

(ii) Area of the figure $= (12 \times 12) + (6 \times 6) + (3 \times 3)$
$$= 144 + 36 + 9 = 189\text{ cm}^2$$

19. *(d)* Side of unshaded portion,

$WX = WV - XV = 15 - 10 = 5\text{ cm}$

Area of $WXQY = 5 \times 3 = 15\text{ cm}^2$

Area of $MNQL = 15 \times 15 = 225\text{ cm}^2$

Area of $WVUT = 225\text{ cm}^2$

$\therefore$ Area of shaded region
$$= (225 - 15) + (225 - 15)$$
$$= 210 + 210 = 420\text{ cm}^2$$

20. *(d)* Given figure,

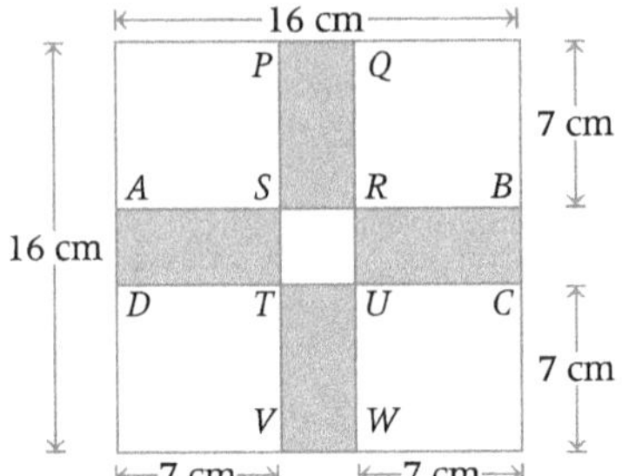

Area of $ASTD = 7 \times 2 = 14\text{ m}^2$

Area of $RBCU = 7 \times 2 = 14\text{ m}^2$

Area of $PQRS = \{16 - (7 + 7)\} \times 7$
$$= (16 - 14) \times 7$$
$$= 2 \times 7 = 14\text{ m}^2$$

Area of $TUWV = $ Area of $PQRS = 14\text{ m}^2$

$\therefore$ Area of shaded region $= 14 + 14 + 14 + 14$
$$= 56\text{ m}^2$$

21. *(b)* Take the figure one by one and find the shaded Areas.

(i)

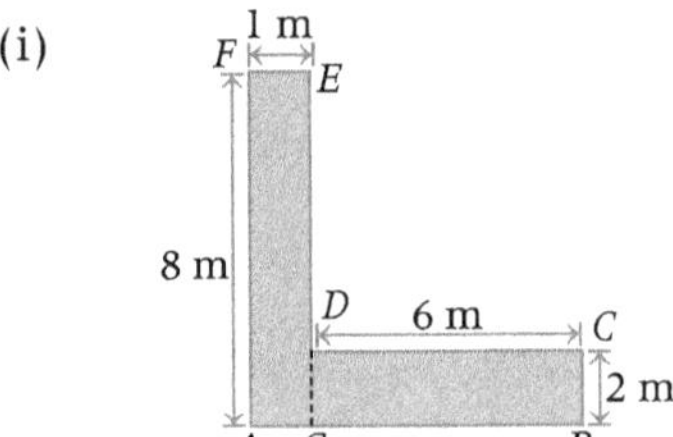

Shaded area of figure = Area of rectangle
$AGEF$ + Area of rectangle $GBCD$
$$= (8 \times 1 + 6 \times 2)\text{ m}^2$$
$$= (8 + 12)\text{ m}$$
$$= 20\text{ m}^2$$

(ii)

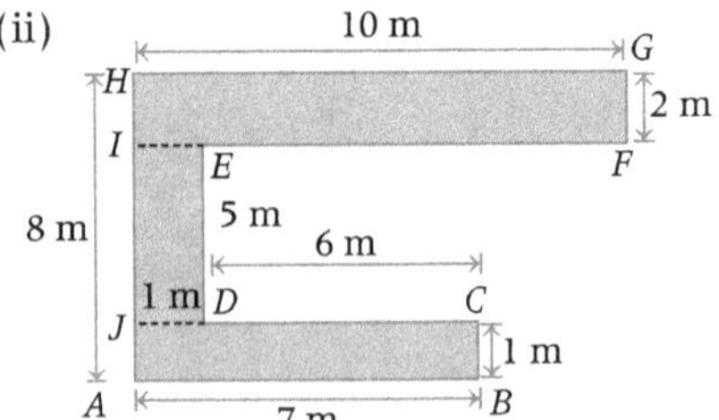

Shaded area of figure = Area of rectangle $ABCJ$ + Area of rectangle $JDEI$ + Area of rectangle $IFGH$

$$= [7 \times 1 + 5 \times 1 + 10 \times 2]\, m^2$$
$$= (7 + 5 + 20)\, m^2 = 32\, m^2$$

(iii)

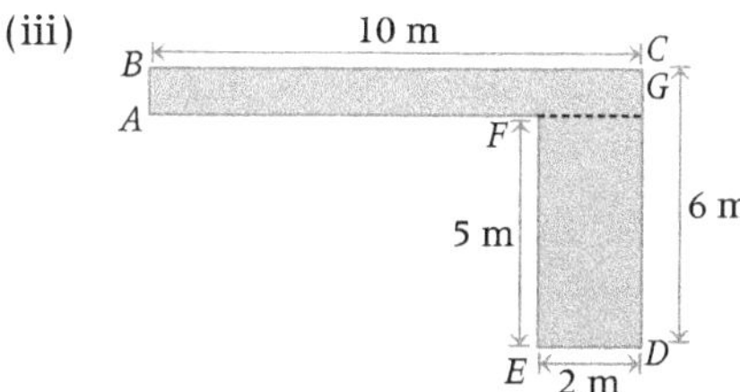

Shaded area of figure = Area of rectangle $ABCG$ + Area of rectangle $EDGF$

$$= [10 \times 1 + 5 \times 2]\, m^2 = 20\, m^2$$

∴ Figure (ii) has maximum shaded area.

22. *(b)* ∵ Anu walks thrice around a square field of side 21 m.

∴ Distance covered by Anu

$$= 3 \times \text{perimeter of square}$$
$$= 3 \times 4 \times 21 = 252\, m$$

∵ Manu walks thrice around a rectangular field of length 10 m and breadth 11 m.

∴ Distance covered by Monu

$$= 3 \times \text{perimeter of rectangular field}$$
$$= 3 \times 2 \times (10 + 11) = 126\, m$$

∴ Anu covers more distance than Manu by

$$= 252 - 126 = 126\, m.$$

23. *(d)* We know that,

Area of a rectangle = length × breadth

$$\therefore \quad 247 = 19 \times P$$
$$\Rightarrow \quad P = \frac{247}{19} = 13\, m$$

Now, from second condition,

$$2(32 + Q) = 98 \qquad [\because \text{Perimeter} = 2(l + b)]$$
$$\Rightarrow \quad 32 + Q = \frac{98}{2} = 49$$
$$\Rightarrow \quad Q = 49 - 32 = 17\, cm$$
$$\text{and} \quad R = 32 \times 17 \qquad [\because \text{Area} = l \times b]$$
$$R = 544\, m^2$$

Chapter 12 : Data Handling

1. *(c)* Number of families having 2 vehicles $= 11$

Number of families having 5 vehicles $= 6$

∴ $11 - 6 = 5$ more families have 2 vehicles than that have 5 vehicles.

Solutions (Q. Nos. 2 and 3) According to the information given in the question,

Colour	Tally marks	No. of Women
Red	||| ||||	9
Brown	||||	4
Green	||||	4
Blue	|||	5
Grey	|||		6
Black	|||	5

2. *(c)* Total number of women who like black and blue colour sarees $= 5 + 5 = 10$

3. *(d)* There are $(9 - 6) = 3$ more women who like red colour saree than grey colour saree.

4. *(d)* Total number of trees in the garden

$$= 15 \times 15 = 225$$

5. *(b)* Total number of mango trees $= 15 \times 8 = 120$

Total number of banana trees $= 15 \times 4 = 60$

∴ The number of mango trees is 2 times the number of banana trees.

6. *(d)* Difference between the numbers of mango trees and banana trees

$$= 15 \times 8 - 15 \times 4 = 120 - 60 = 60$$

Solutions (Q. Nos. 11 and 12) According to the information given in the table,

Transport	Number of people
Bike	$6 \times 13 + 3 = 81$
Bus	$6 \times 6 = 36$
Car	$6 \times 6 = 36$
Walk	$6 \times 3 + 3 = 21$
Bicycle	$6 \times 6 + 3 = 39$

7. *(a)* Number of people not travel by bus and car
$= 81 + 21 + 39 = 141$

8. *(b)* The mode of transport mostly used was bike, hence it is popular.

9. *(b)* From graph, only Dog is with more than 60 families.

10. *(b)* Number of families having Cat $= 40$

Number of families having Parrot $= 60$

$\therefore$ Required difference $= 60 - 40 = 20$

11. *(a)* Height of tallest building $= 90$ m

Height of shortest building $= 30$ m

$\therefore$ Required total height $= (90 + 30)$ m
$= 120$ m

12. *(c)* Number of buildings whose heights are greater than or equal to 50 m but less than 90 m $= 2$ (i.e A and D)

13. *(c)* Marks scored in Maths and Hindi together
$= 120 + 150 = 270$

Marks scored in all subjects
$= 90 + 130 + 100 + 150 + 170 + 120 = 760$

$\therefore$ Required fraction $= \dfrac{270}{760} = \dfrac{27}{76}$

14. *(a)* Marks scored in Science and G.K. together
$= 130 + 100 = 230$

Marks scored in English and Computer together $= 90 + 170 = 260$

$\therefore$ Required difference $= 260 - 230 = 30$

15. *(b)* Number of t-shirts sold in April and July
$= 1600 + 1400 = 3000$

$\because$ Cost of 1 t-shirt $= ₹\ 400$

$\therefore$ Cost of 3000 t-shirts $= ₹\ (400 \times 3000)$
$= ₹\ 1200000$

16. *(d)* Number of t-shirts sold in May and July together $= 1400 + 1400 = 2800$

Number of t-shirt sold in March, June and August together $= 1800 + 1800 + 2000 = 5600$

$\therefore 5600 - 2800 = 2800$ less t-shirts were sold in May and July together than in March, June and August together.

17. *(b)* Total number of employees absent in Accounts $= 10 + 8 = 18$

Total number of employees absent in Editorial
$= 8 + 6 = 14$

Total number of employees absent in Sales
$= 8 + 8 = 16$

Total number of employees absent in Administration $= 6 + 10 = 16$

$\therefore$ Accounts has the maximum number of absent employees.

18. *(c)* Total number of females absent in four departments $= 10 + 8 + 8 + 6 = 32$

Total number of males absent in four departments $= 8 + 6 + 8 + 10 = 32$

$\therefore$ Required ratio $= \dfrac{32}{32} = \dfrac{1}{1}$ or $1 : 1$

19. *(d)* Number of boys passed out from School B $= 2000$

Number of boys passed out from all Schools
$= 1000 + 2000 + 2500 + 2000 + 1000 = 8500$

$\therefore$ Required fraction $= \dfrac{2000}{8500} = \dfrac{4}{17}$

20. *(b)* Number of students passed out from School A $= 1500 + 2500 = 4000$

Number of students passed out from School E
$= 1000 + 500 = 1500$

$\therefore$ Required difference $= 4000 - 1500 = 2500$

21. *(b)*

Days	Number of burgers Sold
Monday	$4 \times 10 = 40$
Tuesday	$5 \times 10 = 50$
Wednesday	$2 \times 10 = 20$
Thursday	$4 \times 10 = 40$
Friday	$6 \times 10 = 60$
Saturday	$7 \times 10 = 70$

(i) On Saturday, the most number of burgers were sold.

(ii) Total number of burgers sold on last two days $= 60 + 70 = 130$

Total number of burgers sold on first four days $= 40 + 50 + 20 + 40 = 150$

$\therefore (150 - 130) = 20$ less burgers were sold on last two days than the first four days.

(iii) Number of burgers sold on Tuesday $= 50$

Cost of 1 burger $= ₹\ 30$

$\therefore$ Total cost of 50 burgers $= ₹ (50 \times 30)$
$$= ₹ 1500$$

22. *(a)* Number of students applied for the competitive exam in 2019 $= 65000$
$\therefore$ Number of symbols required
$$= 65000 \div 500 = 130$$

23. *(b)* Total number of students applied from 2017 to 2021 $= 35000 + 40000 + 65000 + 50000$
$= ₹ 190000$
$\therefore$ Number of symbols required
$= 190000 \div 500 = 380$

24. *(c)* Number of students applied for an in 2016
$$= 35000$$
$\therefore$ Number of symbols required
$$= 35000 \div 500 = 70$$
Number of students applied in 2019 $= 65000$
$\therefore$ Number of symbols required $= 65000 \div 500$
$$= 130$$
$\therefore$ Required symbols $= 130 - 70 = 60$

25. *(a)* Weight of an empty container $= 10 \, \text{gm}$
$$...(i)$$
Weight of container $+$ weight of ball (P, Q and R) $= 45 \, \text{gm}$
$\therefore$ Weight of balls (P, Q and R)
$$= (45 - 10) = 35 \, \text{gm} \qquad ...(ii)$$
Similarly, weight of balls (Q, R and S)
$$= (60 - 10) = 50 \, \text{gm} \qquad ...(iii)$$
Weight fo balls (P, R and S)
$$= (50 - 10) = 40 \, \text{gm} \qquad ...(iv)$$
And, weight of balls (P, Q and S)
$$= (50 - 10) = 40 \, \text{gm} \qquad ...(v)$$
Adding Eqs. (ii), (iii), (iv) and (v), we get
Weight of ball $(3P + 3Q + 3R + 3S)$
$$= (35 + 50 + 40 + 40) \, \text{gm} = 165 \, \text{gm}$$
$\Rightarrow$ Weight of balls $(P + Q + R + S)$
$$= \frac{165}{3} = 55 \, \text{gm} \qquad ...(vi)$$
From Eqs. (iii) and (vi), we have
Weight of ball $P = 55 - 50 = 5 \, \text{gm}$
From Eqs. (iv) and (vi)
weight of ball $Q = 55 - 40 = 15 \, \text{gm}$

$\therefore$ Total weight of balls Q and P
$$= (15 + 5) \, \text{gm}$$
$$= 20 \, \text{gm}$$

Practice Set 1

1. *(d)* Consider an even natural number $= 2$
So, the predecessor of $2 = 2 - 1 = 1$
We get the successor of $2 = 2 + 1 = 3$
Product between them $= 1 \times 3 = 3$
Hence, the product is an odd number.

2. *(b)* It is given that
Side of a square field $= 65 \, \text{m}$
So, the perimeter of square field $= 4 \times$ side of the square
By substituting the values
Perimeter of square field $= 4 \times 65 = 260 \, \text{m}$
Hence, the length of the fence required all around the square field is 260 m.

3. *(c)* 40 tickets of Assam State Lottery were sold by the agent.

4. *(a)* Total number of tickets
$$= \frac{(80 + 50 + 100 + 20 + 40)}{5}$$
$$= \frac{290}{5} = 58$$

5. *(b)* False.
We know that
Maximum vertical length $= 100 \, \text{units}$ (Haryana)
Minimum vertical length $= 20 \, \text{units}$ (Rajasthan)
So, the maximum number of lottery sold for one state is 100 tickets and the minimum is 20 tickets.

6. *(d)*

Number of lines of symmetry in an equilateral triangle $= 3$

7. *(c)* We know that 1 million = 1000000

So, the successor of 1 million
$$= 1000000 + 1 = 1000001$$

8. *(d)* The option (d) is the correct answer.
Many circles can be drawn to pass through two given points.

9. *(b)* Number of cassettes Kavita has = 44

She gives $\dfrac{3}{4}$ of them to Sonia = $\dfrac{3}{4}(44) = 33$

So, the number of cassettes Kavita keeps
$$= 44 - 33 = 11$$

Therefore, Kavita gives 33 cassettes to Sonia and still keeps 11 cassettes.

10. *(a)* Amount given by Radhika's mother = ₹ 10.50
Amount given by Radhika's father = ₹ 15.80
So, the total amount given by her parents
$$= ₹10.50 + ₹15.80 = ₹26.30$$
Hence, the total amount given by her parents is ₹ 26.30.

11. *(c)* Number of boys = 1168

Number of girls = 1095

So, the ratio of the number of boys to that of the girls = 1168 : 1095

Dividing the two terms by their HCF 73

Ratio of number of boys to that of the girls = 16 : 15

Hence, the ratio of the number of boys to that of girls in simplest form is 16 : 15.

12. *(c)* An isosceles trapezium has non-parallel sides equal.

13. *(c)* We know that, the wheel of a bicycle covers 360° in one turn.

It can be written as $\dfrac{360}{90} = 4$ right angles

We know that, in $4\dfrac{1}{2}$ turns the wheel turns by 4

$(4.5) = 18$ right angles

Hence, the number of right angles through which it turns is 18.

14. *(c)* Fraction of wall space painted by Shikha = $\dfrac{1}{5}$

Fraction of wall space painted by Ravish = $\dfrac{3}{5}$

So, the wall space painted by both = $\dfrac{1}{5} + \dfrac{3}{5}$
$$= \dfrac{(1+3)}{5} = \dfrac{4}{5}$$

We get the unpainted space = $\dfrac{(5-4)}{5} = \dfrac{1}{5}$

Therefore, Shikha and Ravish painted $\dfrac{4}{5}$ of the wall space together and the room space left unpainted is $\dfrac{1}{5}$.

15. *(a)* We know that the product of two numbers
= HCF of two numbers × LCM of two numbers
By substituting the values
$1530 = 1\,5 \times$ LCM of two numbers
We get, LCM of two numbers = $\dfrac{1530}{15} = 102$

The option (a) is correct answer.

16. *(c)* It is given that
1st side of triangle = 15 cm
IInd side of triangle = 20 cm
In order to find the length of IIIrd side
We know that, perimeter of a triangle is the sum of all three sides of a triangle
So, the length of 3rd side = perimeter of triangle − sum of length of other two sides
By substituting the values
Length of 3rd side = $50 - (15 + 20) = 15$ cm.
Hence, the length of 3rd side is 15 cm.

17. *(b)*

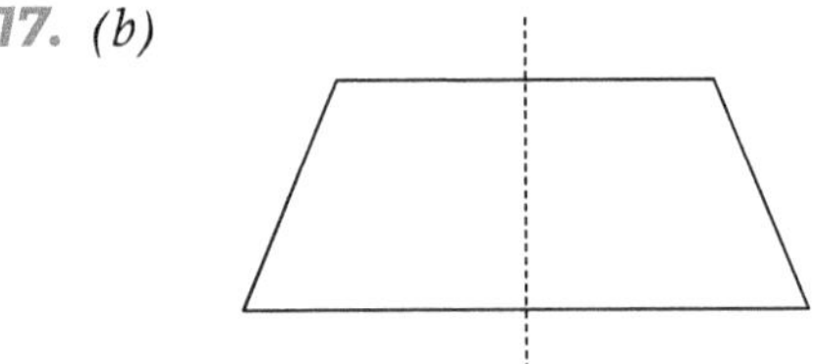

Number of lines of symmetry of Isosceles trapezium
$$= 1$$

18. *(a)* We know that
So, the successor of 99 = 99 + 1 = 100
We get predecessor of 99 = 99 − 1 = 98
Product of them = 100 × 98 = 9800

19. *(c)* We know that, the face value depends on the value of the digit and the place value depends on its place of occurrence.
So, the digits which have same place and face value in a number are the ones digit and zeros of the number.
The given number is 9, 20, 78, 634
We know that 4 which is the ones digit and 0 which is the lakhs digit have same face and place value.

20. *(a)* Number of bulbs shown on Friday = 7

Given that, 1 figure = 2 bulbs
So, the total number of bulbs sold on Friday
$$= 2 \times 7 = 14$$
Hence, 14 bulbs were sold on Friday.

21. *(c)* Number of bulb figures sold on Sunday
$$= 2 \times 9 = 18$$
Given that, Cost of one bulb = ₹ 10
So the total earning on Sunday = $10 \times 18 = $ ₹ 180

22. *(b)* Total bulb figures shown throughout the week
$$= 6 + 8 + 4 + 5 + 7 + 4 + 9 = 43$$
So, the total number of bulbs = $43 \times 2 = 86$
Total earning of the week = $10 \times 86 = $ ₹ 860

23. *(a)* The central angle in a bicycle is 360 which consists of 48 spokes.

So, the angle between a pair of adjacent spokes
$$= \frac{360°}{48} = 7.5$$

Hence, the angle between a pair of adjacent spokes is 7.5.

24. *(b)* Weight of apples bought by Rahul = 4 kg 90 gm
$$= 4.090 \text{ kg}$$
Weight of grapes bought by Rahul = 2 kg 60 gm
$$= 2.060 \text{ kg}$$
Weight of mangoes bought by Rahul = 5 kg 300 gm
$$= 5.300 \text{ kg}$$
So the weight of all the fruits
$$= 4.090 + 2.060 + 5.300 = 11.450 \text{kg}$$
Hence, the weight of the fruits bought by Rahul is 11.450 kg

25. *(c)* It is given that
Length of a steel tape = 10 m
Width of steel tape = 2.4 cm
So, the ratio of its length to width = 10 m / 2.4 cm
We know that, 1 m = 100 cm
Ratio of its length to width = 1000 cm/2.4 cm
Dividing the two terms by HCF 0.8 cm
Ratio of its length to width = 1250 : 3
Hence, the ratio of its length to width is 1250 : 3.

26. *(c)* A quadrilateral having two pairs of equal adjacent sides but unequal opposite sides is called a kite.

27. *(a)* Only 1 circle can be drawn to pass through three non-collinear points.
The option (a) is the correct answer.

28. *(a)* Sugar bought by Ramesh = $2\frac{1}{2}$ kg

It can be written as
Sugar bought by Ramesh = $\frac{(2 \times 2) + 1)}{2} = \frac{5}{2}$ kg

Sugar bought by Rohit = $3\frac{1}{2}$ kg

It can be written as
Sugar bought by Rohit = $\frac{(2 \times 3) + 1}{2}$
$$= \frac{7}{2} \text{ kg}$$

So, the total sugar bought by both of them = Sugar bought by Ramesh + Sugar bought by Rohit
By substituting the values
Total sugar bought by both of them
$$= \frac{5}{2} + \frac{7}{2} = \frac{12}{2} = 6 \text{ kg}$$

Therefore, the total amount of sugar bought by both of them is 6 kg.

29. *(b)* We know that the LCM of 15, 20, 24 and 32 is
$$15 = 3 \times 5 = 3^1 \times 5^1$$
$$20 = 2 \times 2 \times 5 = 2^2 \times 5^1$$
$$24 = 2 \times 2 \times 2 \times 3 = 2^3 \times 3^1$$
$$32 = 2 \times 2 \times 2 \times 2 \times 2 = 2^5$$
So, the LCM = $25 \times 31 \times 51 = 480$
The option (b) is correct answer.

30. *(d)* It is given that
Each side of a square field = 100 m
We can find, the wire required to fence the square field by determining the perimeter = 4 × each side of a square field
By substituting the values
Perimeter of the square field = $4 \times 100 = 400$ m
So, the length of wire which is required to fence three layers is = $3 \times 400 = 1200$ m
Hence, the length of wire needed to fence three layers is 1200 m.

31. *(d)*

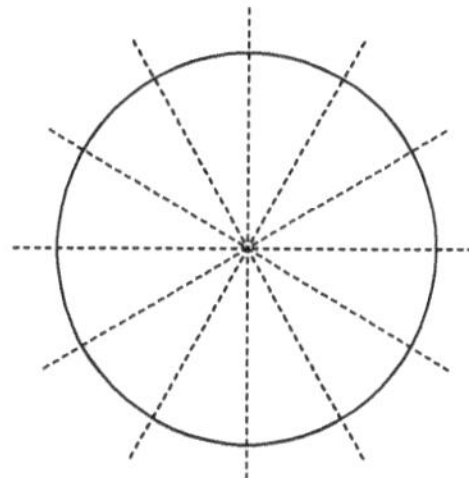

Number of lines of symmetry in circle = infinite.

32. *(c)* We know that, the set of numbers which has common factor as 1 are called co-prime.

So, the LCM of two co-prime numbers and their product are equal.

The option (c) is correct answer.

33. *(d)* The place value of first seven is $7 \times 100 = 700$

The place value of second seven is

$$7 \times 1000000 = 7000000$$

So, the required difference

$$= 7000000 - 700 = 6999300$$

Therefore, the difference of the place values of two 7's in 257839705 is 6999300.

34. *(c)* A reflex angle measures more than $180°$ but less than $360°$.

The option (c) is the correct answer.

35. *(c)* Cloth bought by Nasreen for shirt = 3m 20 cm

$$= 3.20 \text{ m}$$

Cloth bought by Nasreen for skirt = 2m 50 cm

$$= 2.05 \text{ m}$$

So, the total cloth bought by her

$$= 3.20 + 2.05 = 5.25 \text{ m} = 5 \text{ m } 25 \text{ cm}$$

Hence, the total cloth bought by her is 5 m 25 cm.

36. *(c)* Duration of office = 9 am to 5 pm = 8 h

Lunch interval = 30 min

So, the ratio of lunch interval to the period in office

$$= 30 \text{min}/8 \text{ h}$$

We know that, 1 h = 60 min.

Ratio of lunch interval to the period in office

$$= \frac{30}{(8 \times 60)} = \frac{30}{480}$$

Dividing the two terms by HCF 30

Ratio of lunch interval to the period in office

$$= \left(\frac{30}{480}\right) \times \left(\frac{30}{30}\right) = 1:16$$

Hence, the ratio of lunch interval to the total period in office is 1 : 16.

37. *(c)* We know that,

Fraction of book teacher taught $= \dfrac{3}{5}$

Fraction of book Vivek revised $= \dfrac{1}{5}$

So, the fraction of book Vivek still have to revise

$$= \frac{3}{5} - \frac{1}{5} = \frac{(3-1)}{5} = \frac{2}{5}$$

Hence, Vivek still have to revise 2/5 of the book.

38. *(d)* We know that, the factors of

$$91 = 1 \times 7 \times 13$$
$$81 = 1 \times 3 \times 3 \times 3 \times 3$$
$$87 = 1 \times 3 \times 29$$
$$97 = 1 \times 97$$

Hence, 81, 87 and 91 are not prime numbers.

The option (d) is correct answer.

39. *(b)* It is given that

Shikha runs around a square of side = 75 m

So, the perimeter = $4 \times 75 = 300$ m

Priya runs around a rectangle having

Length = 60 m

Breadth = 45 m

So, the distance covered can be found from the perimeter = $2(L + B)$

By substituting the values

Perimeter = $2(60 + 45) = 2 \times 105 = 210$ m

Difference in the distance covered

$$= 300 \text{ m} - 210 \text{ m} = 90 \text{ m}$$

Hence, Priya covers the smaller distance by 90 m.

40. *(b)* The number of lines of symmetry of a kite is 1.

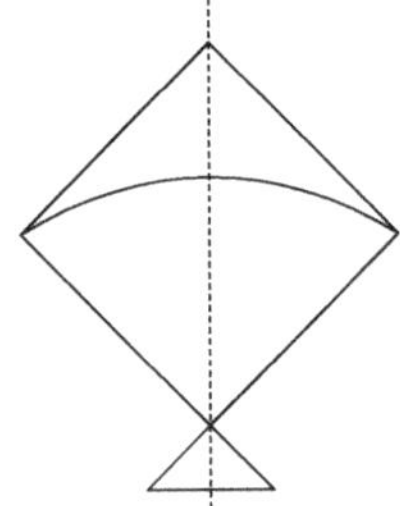

The option (b) is the correct answer.

41. *(a)* The dimensions of garden are

Length = 70 m

Breadth = 50 m

So, the perimeter = $2(L + B)$

By substituting the values

Perimeter = $2(70 + 50) = 2 \times 120 = 240$ m

Given,

Arvind fixes a post every 5 m apart

Number of posts required $= \dfrac{240}{5} = 48$

The length of each post = 2 m

So, the total length of the pipe required

$$= 48 \times 2 = 96 \text{ m}$$

Hence, the total length of the pipes he bought for the posts is 96 m.

42. *(c)* We know that, the set of numbers which has common factor as 1 are called co-prime.

LCM of two co-prime numbers and their product is equal.

So, the HCF of two co-prime numbers is 1

The option (c) is correct answer.

43. *(b)* Let number of books be x.

$\therefore$ Number of pens $= x - 5$

According to the question,

$$4x + 25(x - 5) = 107$$
$$\Rightarrow \quad 4x + 25x - 125 = 107$$
$$\Rightarrow \quad 29x = 107 + 125$$
$$\Rightarrow \quad 29x = 232$$
$$\Rightarrow \quad x = 8$$

44. *(c)* We know,

$$A : 48 = 2 \times 3 \times 8$$
$$B : 15 = 4 + 5 + 6$$
$$K : 63 = 1 \times 7 \times 9$$

$\therefore$ The largest number in the cards of Katrina is 9.

45. *(d)* Let number of nailpaints Kareena has be x.

$\therefore$ Number of nailpaints given to Mala

$$= \frac{1}{3}x + 10$$

Remaining number of nailpaints $= \frac{2}{3}x - 10$

Number of nailpaints given to Ankita

$$= \frac{3}{4}\left(\frac{2}{3}x - 10\right) - 1$$
$$= \frac{1}{2}x - \frac{15}{2} - 1 = \frac{1}{2}x - \frac{17}{2}$$

Remaining number of nailpaints

$$= \frac{2}{3}x - 10 - \left(\frac{1}{2}x - \frac{17}{2}\right)$$
$$= \frac{2}{3}x - \frac{1}{2}x - 10 + \frac{17}{2} = \frac{1}{6}x - \frac{3}{2}$$

So, $\frac{1}{6}x - \frac{3}{2} = 30$

$$\Rightarrow \quad \frac{1}{6}x = 30 + \frac{3}{2}$$
$$\Rightarrow \quad \frac{1}{6}x = \frac{60 + 3}{2}$$
$$\Rightarrow \quad \frac{1}{6}x = \frac{63}{2}$$
$$\Rightarrow \quad x = \frac{63}{2} \times 6$$
$$\Rightarrow \quad x = 63 \times 3$$
$$\Rightarrow \quad x = 189$$

46. *(d)*

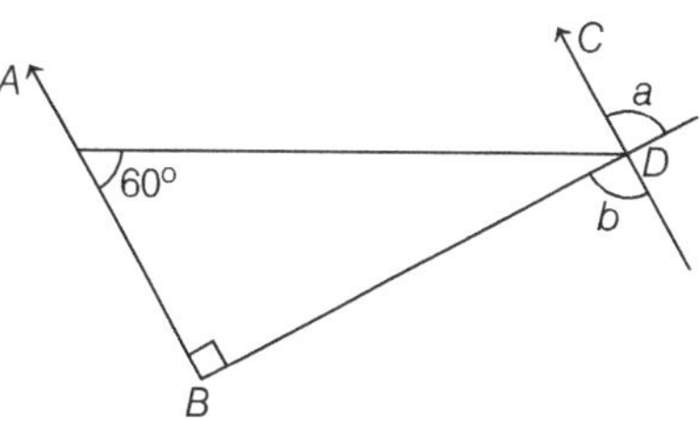

Given, $AB \parallel CD$

$\therefore \qquad \angle ABD + \angle CDB = 180°$

[angles on same side of transversal]

$\therefore \qquad \angle CDB = 90°$ $\qquad$ [$\angle ABD = 90°$]

Now, $\angle a + \angle CDB = 180°$ $\qquad$ [linear pair]

$\therefore \qquad \angle a + 90° = 180°$

$\Rightarrow \qquad \angle a = 90°$

Also, $\qquad \angle a = \angle b$

[$\because$ vertically opposite angles]

$\therefore \qquad \angle a + \angle b = 90° + 90°$
$$= 180°$$

47. *(a)* 1. False, $(-4) > (-10)$, hence, -4 will be on the right side of the -10 on the number line.

$$(-4) > (-10).$$

2. False, -100 is smaller than -50.

Hence, $-50 > -100$

3. True.

4. True.

48. *(a)* Figure (a) has the smallest perimeter

Perimeter of a closed figure is the distance covered in one round along the boundary of the figure

We know that, perimeter of figure = numbers of sides × length of each sides

Consider the given figures,

(a) figure (a) has 10 units and each side have length 1 cm

So, perimeter $= 10 \times 1 = 10$ cm

(b) figure (b) has 12 units and each side have length 1 cm

So, perimeter $= 12 \times 1 = 12$ cm

(c) figure (c) has 14 sides and each side have length 1 cm

So, perimeter $= 14 \times 1 = 14$ cm

(d) figure (d) has 14 sides and each side have length 1 cm

So, perimeter $= 14 \times 1 = 14$ cm

By comparing all the perimeters of given figures, figure (a) has smallest perimeter.

49. *(c)* All the options given in the question are further simplified as,

(a) $\dfrac{6}{8}$

Divide both numerator and denominator by 2. $= \dfrac{3}{4}$

(b) $\dfrac{12}{16}$

Divide both numerator and denominator by 4.

$$= \dfrac{3}{4}$$

(c) $\dfrac{15}{25}$

Divide both numerator and denominator by 5.

$$= \dfrac{3}{5}$$

(d) $\dfrac{18}{24}$

Divide both numerator and denominator by 6.

$$= \dfrac{3}{4}$$

Comparing all results, $\left(\dfrac{3}{4} = \dfrac{3}{4} = \dfrac{3}{4}\right) \neq \dfrac{3}{5}$

Therefore, $\left(\dfrac{6}{8} = \dfrac{12}{16} = \dfrac{18}{24}\right) \neq \dfrac{15}{25}$

50. *(d)* From the question it is given that A, B, G, M and O stand for the fruits Apple, Banana, Grapes, Mango and Orange respectively.

So, by observing the choices of the fruits of 42 students in a class Banana (B) and Grapes (G) are liked by an equal number of students i.e. 8 students each.

Practice Set 2

1. *(a)* Number of books bought $= 8m + 5n$

Cost of $1m$ book $= ₹\ 26.75$

Cost of $1\ n$ book $= ₹\ 35.75$

$\therefore$ Total cost $= 8(25.75) + 5(35.75)$

$$= 206 + 178.75$$
$$= ₹\ 384.75$$

2. *(d)* Consider, $9 + [9z - \{6 + 3y - (2z - 3y) - 3\}]$

$$= 9 + [9z - \{6 + 3y - 2z + 3y - 3\}]$$
$$= 9 + [9z - 6 - 3y + 2z - 3y + 3]$$
$$= 9 + 9z - 6 - 3y + 2z - 3y + 3$$
$$= 9 + 3 - 6 + 9z + 2z - 3y - 3y$$
$$= 6 + 11z - 6y$$

3. *(c)* Quantity of juice = 5 liter and 500 mL

$$= 5000\,\text{mL} + 500\,\text{mL} \qquad [\because 1\ \text{liter} = 1000\,\text{mL}]$$
$$= 5500\ \text{mL}$$

Capacity of one glass $= 25\,\text{mL}$

$\therefore$ Number of glasses it can fill $= \dfrac{5500}{25} = 220$

4. *(a)* We have,

$$\frac{4}{12} = \frac{10}{30} = \frac{15}{x} = \frac{y}{54} = \frac{24}{z}$$

So, $\qquad \dfrac{4}{12} = \dfrac{15}{x}$

$\Rightarrow \qquad x = \dfrac{15 \times 12}{4}$

$\Rightarrow \qquad x = 45$

and $\qquad \dfrac{4}{12} = \dfrac{y}{54} = y = \dfrac{54 \times 4}{12}$

$\Rightarrow \qquad y = 18$

Also, $\qquad \dfrac{4}{12} = \dfrac{24}{z}$

$\Rightarrow \qquad z = \dfrac{12 \times 24}{4}$

$\Rightarrow \qquad z = 72$

5. *(b)* Consider $(ab - ac) \div abc$

For $a = 2, b = 4$ and $c = -1$

$\{(2 \times 4) - (2 \times (-1))\} \div 2 \times 4 \times (-1)$

$$= \{8 + 2\} \div (-8)$$
$$= \dfrac{10}{-8} = -\dfrac{5}{4}$$

6. *(d)* Here, $= 2\dfrac{3}{12} - 1\dfrac{2}{4}$

$$= \dfrac{27}{12} - \dfrac{6}{4}$$
$$= \dfrac{27}{12} - \dfrac{18}{12} = \dfrac{9}{12}$$

7. *(b)* LCM must be divisible by HCF.

8. *(d)* The line which divides a circle equal is called diameter.

9. *(a)* Let star fish be denoted by S and gold fish by G.

$\therefore \qquad S : G = 3 : 7$

$\Rightarrow \qquad S = \dfrac{3}{7}G$

$\therefore$ We have,

$$\dfrac{S}{G + 25} = \dfrac{6}{19}$$

$\Rightarrow \qquad 19\,S = 6\,G + 150$

$$\Rightarrow \qquad 19 \times \frac{3}{7} G = 6G + 150$$

$$\Rightarrow \qquad 57G = 42G + 150 \times 7$$

$$\Rightarrow \qquad 15G = 150 \times 7$$

$$\Rightarrow \qquad G = 70$$

$$\therefore \qquad S = \frac{3}{7} \times 70 = 30$$

10. *(c)* Consider 700900800

Seventy crore nine lakh and eight hundred

11. *(a)* Consider $\left(\frac{2}{3} \text{ of } 16\right) - \left(\frac{1}{18} \div \frac{1}{3}\right)$

$$\Rightarrow \qquad \left(\frac{2}{3} \times 16\right) - \left(\frac{1}{18} \times 3\right)$$

$$\Rightarrow \qquad \left(\frac{32}{3}\right) - \left(\frac{1}{6}\right)$$

$$\Rightarrow \qquad \frac{64 - 1}{6} \qquad [\because \text{LCM of 3 and 6 = 6}]$$

$$= \frac{63}{6} = \frac{21}{2} = 10\frac{1}{2}$$

12. *(b)* Required volume = HCF (145, 116)

$$= \text{HCF } (5 \times 29, 2 \times 2 \times 29)$$

$$= 29 \text{ liters}$$

13. *(a)* Given, 27432* must be divisible by 6.

So, 27432* must be divisible by 2 and 3.

to be divisible by 2, * = 2, 4, 6, 8, 0

to be divisible by 3,

$2 + 7 + 4 + 3 + 2 + $* must be divisible by 3.

i.e. $18 + $* must be divisible by 3.

$$\therefore \qquad * = 0, 6$$

Now, $\qquad 0 < 6$

$$* = 0$$

14. *(a)* Average of scores $= \dfrac{a + b + c}{3} \times 100$

$$= \left(\frac{a}{3} + \frac{b}{3} + \frac{c}{3}\right) \times 100$$

15. *(d)* None of them is divisible by 11.

16. *(d)* Given, $\angle AOB$ is a right angle,

$$\therefore x + 20° + 2x + 10° = 90°$$

$$\Rightarrow \qquad 3x + 30° = 90°$$

$$\Rightarrow \qquad 3x = 60°$$

$$\Rightarrow \qquad x = 20°$$

$$\therefore \qquad \angle AOC = x + 20°$$

$$= 20° + 20° = 40°$$

and $\qquad \angle COB = 2x + 10°$

$$= 2 \times 20° + 10° = 50°$$

17. *(b)* Given, $a \Delta b = 7 \times a - 3 \times b$

Consider $6 \Delta 4 = 7 \times 6 - 3 \times 4 \qquad [\because a = 6, b = 4]$

$$= 42 - 12 = 30$$

18. *(b)* We have, $(30 - 24) = 6$, $(35 - 29) = 6$,

$(45 - 39) = 6$ and $(50 - 44) = 6$

$\therefore$ The required number = LCM (30, 35, 45, 50) − 6

$$= 3150 - 6 = 3144$$

19. *(a)* According to the question,

$$0.2x + 600 = 0.5x$$

$$\Rightarrow \qquad \frac{1}{5}x + 600 = \frac{1}{2}x$$

$$\Rightarrow \qquad 600 = \frac{3x}{10}$$

$$\Rightarrow \qquad x = 2000 \text{ mL}$$

$$= 2 \text{ liters} \qquad [\because 1 \text{ liter} = 1000 \text{ mL}]$$

20. *(c)* Consider

$$4x + 6z - (x + 3y - 3x) + 5y$$

$$= 4x + 6z - x - 3y + 3x + 5y$$

$$= 6x + 6z + 2y$$

$$= 6 \times 2 + 6 \times (-2) + 2 \times 3$$

$$[\text{put } x = 2, y = 3 \text{ and } z = -2]$$

$$= 12 - 12 + 6 = 6$$

21. *(a)* Given,

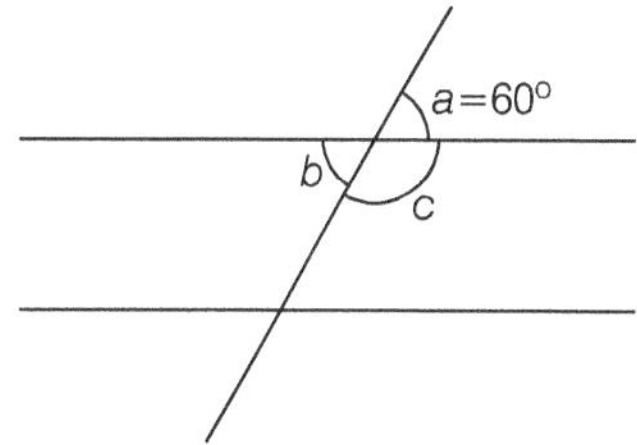

We know, $\angle a = \angle b \qquad$ [vertically opposite angles]

$$\therefore \qquad \angle b = 60°$$

Now, $\angle b + \angle c = 180° \qquad$ [linear pair]

$$\therefore \qquad \angle c = 180° - \angle b$$

$$= 180° - 60° = 120°$$

22. *(c)* If number is divisible by two co-prime numbers, then it is divisible by their product.

23. *(c)* Time taken by 30 persons to consume 240 kg of rice = 4 days

Let time taken by 40 persons to consume 240 kg of rice = x days.

We have,

$$\frac{30 \times 4}{48} = \frac{40 \times x}{240}$$

$$\Rightarrow \quad \frac{30 \times 4 \times 240}{48 \times 40} = x$$

$$x = 15 \text{ days}$$

24. *(c)* Let the smaller angle be x.

$\therefore$ We have,

$$x + x + 40^\circ = 180^\circ$$
$$\Rightarrow \qquad 2x = 140^\circ$$
$$\Rightarrow \qquad x = 70^\circ$$

$\therefore$ The angle is $70 + 40 = 110^\circ$

25. *(b)* Largest number formed = 8520

Smallest number formed = 2058

$\therefore$ Difference = $8520 - 2058 = 6462$

26. *(b)* $\text{SI} = \dfrac{P \times R \times T}{100}$

$$= \frac{300 \times 15 \times 20}{100 \times 12}$$

$$= ₹\, 75$$

27. *(c)* 970429

$$= 9 \times 100000 + 7 \times 10000 + 0 + 4$$
$$\times 100 + 2 \times 10 + 9 \times 1$$

28. *(a)* Consider

$$52 - [2 - 3\{4 + (7 - 8) - \overline{2 + 7}\} - 4]$$
$$= 52 - [2 - 3\{4 - 1 - 9\} - 4]$$
$$= 52 - [2 - 3\{-6\} - 4]$$
$$= 52 - [2 + 18 - 4]$$
$$= 52 - [16]$$
$$= 52 - 16 = 36$$

29. *(b)*

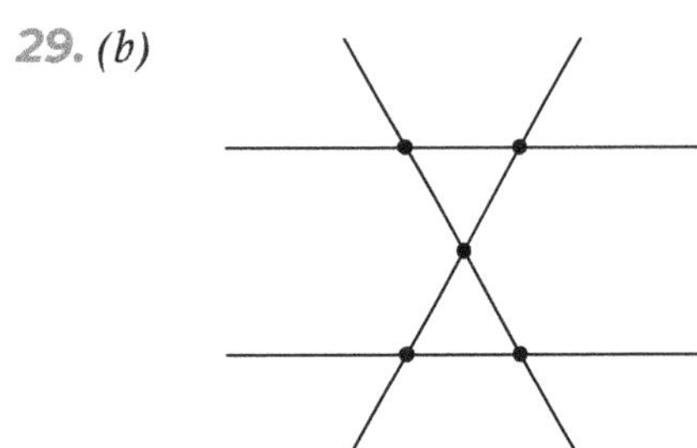

There are 5 points of intersection.

30. *(b)* Let x must be added.

$\therefore$ We have,

$$\frac{7 + x}{16 + x} = \frac{43 + x}{79 + x}$$

$$\Rightarrow 553 + 86x + x^2 = 688 + 59x + x^2$$
$$\Rightarrow \qquad 27x = 135 \quad \Rightarrow \quad x = 5$$

31. *(b)* According to the question,

$$10 : 1500 :: x : 75000$$

$\therefore$ We get,

$$\frac{10}{1500} = \frac{x}{75000}$$
$$\Rightarrow \qquad \frac{10 \times 75000}{1500} = x$$
$$\Rightarrow \qquad x = 500$$

32. *(a)* The required number = LCM (8, 20, 24) + 7

$$= 120 + 7 = 127$$

33. *(c)* A Reflex angle measures more than 180° but less than 360°.

34. *(b)* According to the question,

$$2x + 2x + 2 + 2x + 4 = 30$$
$$\Rightarrow \qquad 6x + 6 = 30$$
$$\Rightarrow \qquad 6x = 24 \quad \Rightarrow \quad x = 4$$

So, the numbers are 8, 10 and 12.

35. *(d)* Consider

$$(-182) + (-30) + 6 + (-721) - (+432) + 700 - (-17)$$
$$\Rightarrow -182 - 30 + 6 - 721 - 432 + 700 + 17$$
$$\Rightarrow -182 - 30 - 721 - 432 + 6 + 700 + 17$$
$$\Rightarrow -1365 + 723 = -642$$

36. *(a)* Required length of tape

$$= \text{HCF of } (825, 675, 450) = 75 \text{cm}$$

37. *(c)* Number of diagonals in a polygon

$$= \frac{n(n - 3)}{2}$$

Number of sides in octagon are 8 i.e. $n = 8$

$$\frac{8(8 - 3)}{2} = \frac{8 \times 5}{2} = 20$$

$\therefore$ Number of diagonals in a octagon = 20

38. *(a)* We have,

$$6x = 1 \times 2 \times 3 \times 4 \times 5 \times 6 = 720$$

39. *(c)* Given, $u \, \nabla \, v = \dfrac{10}{u} - \dfrac{12}{v}$

So, $3 \, \nabla \, 7 = \dfrac{10}{3} - \dfrac{12}{7} = \dfrac{70 - 36}{21} = \dfrac{34}{21}$

40. *(c)* Let x be the total amount.

So, $0.3x + 0.4x + 40 + 50 = x$

$$\Rightarrow \qquad 0.7x + 90 = x$$
$$\Rightarrow \qquad 90 = 0.3x$$
$$\Rightarrow \qquad x = \frac{900}{3}$$
$$\Rightarrow \qquad x = 300$$

$\therefore$ Neel spent altogether on Monday and Tuesday
$$= 300 \times (0.3 + 0.4)$$
$$= 300 \times 0.7 = ₹\,210$$

41. *(c)* Given $X : Y = 4 : 1$

$\Rightarrow \qquad X = 4Y$

and $\qquad \dfrac{X - 39}{Y + 39} = \dfrac{7}{5}$

$\Rightarrow \qquad 5X - 195 = 7Y + 273$

$\Rightarrow \qquad 20Y - 195 = 7Y + 273$

$\qquad\qquad 13Y = 468$

$\qquad\qquad Y = 36$

$\qquad\qquad X = 4 \times 36 = 144$

$\Rightarrow \qquad X + Y = 144 + 36 = 180$

$\therefore$ Total weight $= 180$

42. *(d)* To be divisible by 4 and 25, last two digits must be 00.

$\therefore \quad \bigcirc = 0$ and $\boxed{\bigcirc}$

To be divisible by 3,

$3 + 6 + 8 + x + 0 + 0$ must be divisible by 3.

$17 + x$ must be divisible by 3.

$\therefore x = 1 \qquad\qquad$ [$\because 18$ is divisible 3]

So, $\boxtimes = 1$

43. *(d)* Statements in option (a), option (b), option (c) are correct.

Hence, option (d) is correct.

44. *(c)* In the given figure, COD is a straight line and $\angle AOD = 120°$

$\therefore \angle AOC + \angle AOD = 180°$ [linear pair]

$\Rightarrow \qquad \angle AOC = 180° - 120°$

$\qquad\qquad = 60°$

Now, $EO \perp AB$,

$\Rightarrow \qquad \angle EOA = 90°$

$\Rightarrow \quad \angle EOC + \angle COA = 90°$

$\Rightarrow \qquad \angle EOC = 90° - 60° = 30°$

$\Rightarrow \qquad \angle BOD = \angle AOC = 60°$

$\qquad\qquad$ [vertically opposite angles]

Now, $FQ \perp CD$,

$\Rightarrow \qquad \angle FOD = 90°$

$\Rightarrow \quad \angle FOB + \angle BOD = 90°$

$\Rightarrow \quad \angle FOB = 90° - 60° = 30°$

Now, AB is a straight line,

$\therefore \quad \angle BOF + \angle EOF + \angle EOA = 180°$ [linear pair]

$\therefore \qquad \angle EOF = 180° - 90° - 30°$

$\qquad\qquad = 60°$

45. *(d)* Consider $\dfrac{\dfrac{2}{5} + \dfrac{1}{4}}{\dfrac{3}{8} \times \dfrac{4}{5} - 1\dfrac{9}{10}}$

$\Rightarrow \quad \dfrac{\dfrac{8 + 5}{20}}{\dfrac{3}{10} - \dfrac{19}{10}} \Rightarrow \dfrac{\dfrac{13}{20}}{\dfrac{-16}{10}}$

$\Rightarrow \quad \dfrac{13}{20} \times -\dfrac{10}{16} \Rightarrow -\dfrac{13}{32}$

46. *(a)* Consider

$- 4 + 3\,[24 - (- 25) \times 8 \div (- 1.8 - 0.2)]$
$$= - 4 + 3[24 + 25 \times 8 \div (-2)]$$
$$= - 4 + 3\,[24 + 25 \times - 4]$$
$$= - 4 + 3\,[24 - 10]$$
$$= - 4 + 3[14]$$
$$= - 4 + 42 = 38$$

47. *(c)*

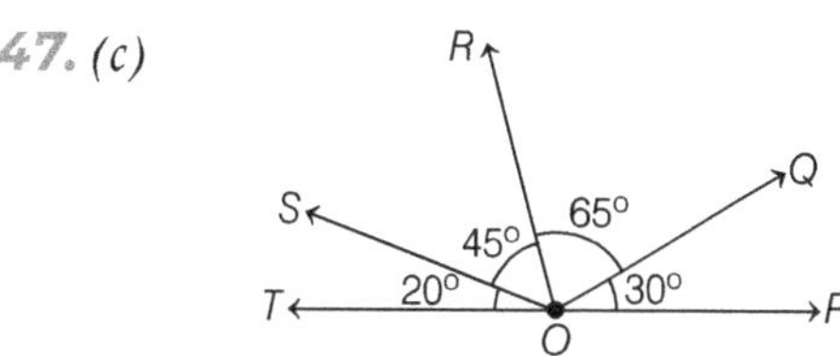

Obtuse angle is defined as an angle formed is greater than 90° and less than 180°.

From the above figure,

Obtuse angle are, $\angle ROP = \angle ROQ + \angle QOP$

$\qquad\qquad = 65° + 30° = 95°$

$\angle SOP = \angle ROQ + \angle QOP + \angle SOR$

$\qquad\qquad = 65° + 30° + 45° = 140°$

$\angle SOQ = \angle SOR + \angle ROQ$

$\qquad\qquad = 45° + 65° = 110°$

$\angle TOQ = \angle TOS + \angle SOR + \angle ROQ$

$\qquad\qquad = 20° + 45° + 65°$

$\qquad\qquad = 130°$

Therefore, number of obtuse angle formed are 4.

48. *(a)* From option (a) Perimeter remains same but area changes.

We know that, area of big rectangle

$\qquad = $ length $\times$ breadth

$\qquad = 10 \times 20 = 200\,\text{cm}^2$

Area of small rectangle $= 5 \times 2$

$\qquad\qquad = 10\,\text{cm}^2$

Perimeter of rectangle $= 2$ (length + breadth)

$\qquad\qquad = 2(20 + 10)$

$\qquad\qquad = 2 \times 30$

$\qquad\qquad = 60\,\text{cm}$

Then, perimeter of new figure
$$= 20 + 8 + 5 + 2 + 15 + 10$$
$$= 60 \text{ cm}$$

Area of new figure = Area of big rectangle − Area of new figure $= 200 - 10 = 190 \text{ cm}^2$

By comparing all the results, perimeter remains same but area changes.

49. *(a)* From the question it is given that,

Savitri has a sum of ₹ x

She spent money on grocery = ₹ 1000

She spent money on clothes = ₹ 500

She spent money on education = ₹ 400

She received gift = ₹ 200

Total money spent by Savitri
$$= 1000 + 500 + 400 = ₹ 1900$$

Then,

Total money left with her after deducting
$$= ₹ (x - 1900)$$

Therefore, money left with her after adding gift money $= (x - 1900) + 200 = x - 1700$

50. *(c)* Saturn and Jupiter take 9 h 56 min and 10 h 40 min, respectively for one spin on their axes.

The ratio of the time taken by Saturn and Jupiter in lowest form is 149 : 160.

From the question,

Saturn takes 9 h 56 min for one spin on their axes

We know that, 1 h = 60 min

So, $(9 \times 60) + 56$
$$= 540 + 56 = 596 \text{ min}$$

Jupiter takes 10 h 40 min for one spin on their axes
$$= (10 \times 60) + 40$$
$$= 600 + 40$$
$$= 640 \text{ min}$$

The ratio of the time taken by Saturn and Jupiter in lowest form is $= \dfrac{596}{640}$

Divide both numerator and denominator by 2,
$$= \dfrac{298}{320}$$

Again, divide both numerator and denominator by 2,
$$= \dfrac{149}{160}$$

Therefore, the ratio of the time taken by Saturn and Jupiter in lowest form is 149 : 160.